TABLE OF CONTENTS

I.   INTRODUCTION...1
      A.   MAJOR RESEARCH QUESTION..1
      B.   IMPORTANCE..1
      C.   PROBLEMS AND HYPOTHESES 2
      D.   LITERATURE REVIEW 3
            1.   Introduction..3
            2.   Affected Nation Absorptive Capacity and Appropriateness of
                  Force...5
      E.   METHODS AND SOURCES 7
      F.   THESIS OVERVIEW 9

II.   HUMANITARIAN DISASTER PARADIGMS 11
      A.   INTRODUCTION..11
      B.   NORMS AND GUIDANCE 11
            1.   Oslo Guidelines and OCHA 12
            2.   Observed Trends and Practices..15
            3.   U.S. Military Trends and Practices within Disaster Relief...........19
                  a.   OHDACA Considerations...22
            4.   Predictive Variables within FHA Assessments 23
                  a.   Development of Civil Relief Institutions...............................25
                  b.   Organic Military Capabilities...25
      C.   CONCLUSION 26

III. JAPAN EARTHQUAKE AND TSUNAMI (2011) 27
      A.   INTRODUCTION..27
      B.   SCOPE OF THE DISASTER 27
      C.   U.S. RESPONSE 28
            1.   Coordination with USAID...32
      D.   PREDICTIVE VARIABLES 34
            1.   Civil Relief Institutions...34
            2.   Host Nation Military Capabilities 36
      E.   CONCLUSION 37

IV.   NORTHERN INDONESIA EARTHQUAKE AND TSUNAMI (2004)................39
      A.   INTRODUCTION..39
      B.   SCOPE OF THE DISASTER 40
      C.   U.S. RESPONSE 42
            1.   Coordination with USAID...47
      D.   PREDICTIVE VARIABLES 48
            1.   Civil Relief Institutions...49
            2.   Host Nation Military Capabilities 50
      E.   CONCLUSION 52

V.   CONCLUDING REMARKS 55

A.   INTRODUCTION...55
B.   ANALYSIS AND KEY FINDINGS 55
    1.   Value of Predictive Variables 57
    2.   U.S. Maritime Forces as the Primary Agent for Relief 58
    3.   U.S. Navy and Japanese Maritime Self-Defense Force
        Familiarity 59
C.   U.S. SECURITY POLICY RECOMMENDATIONS 60
D.   RESEARCH OVERVIEW..62
    1.   Significance Revisited 62
    2.   Research Shortfalls 62
    3.   Areas for Future Study..63

LIST OF REFERENCES...65

LIST OF FIGURES

Figure 1.   Interagency Coordination Flow (From Joint Publication 3–29, 2009). 21
Figure 2.   Operation Tomodachi Task Organization (From USFJ TASKORD 1 to OPORD 11–01 150845ZMAR11) 29
Figure 3.   MITAM Data from Operation Tomodachi (From USAID OFDA DART Lead, 09/20/2012). 33
Figure 4.   Map of IDP Distribution (From Human Rights Center, 2005). 41
Figure 5.   CSF-536 Task Organization (From Office of History, Pacific Air Forces, 2005). 44

THIS PAGE INTENTIONALLY LEFT BLANK

LIST OF TABLES

Table 1.   Self-Defense Force Statistics (From Japan's Ministry of Defense   White Paper, 2012). 37

THIS PAGE INTENTIONALLY LEFT BLANK

LIST OF ACRONYMS AND ABBREVIATIONS

AOR	Area of Operation
APC-MADRO	Asia-Pacific Military Assistance to Disaster Relief Operations
BAKORNAS PBP	Badan Koordinasi Nasional Penanggulangan Bencana dan Penanganan Pengungsi
COM	Chief of Mission
DART	Disaster Assistance Response Team
DoD	Department of Defense
DoS	Department of State
DSCA	Defense Security Cooperation Agency
FHA	Foreign Humanitarian Assistance
HA	Humanitarian Assistance
HAST	Humanitarian Assistance Survey Team
HMA	Humanitarian Mine Action
IDRA	International Disaster Relief Assistance
JIPOE	Joint Intelligence Preparation of the Operational Environment
JFMCC	Joint Forces Maritime Component Commander
JRCS	Japanese Red Cross Society
JGSDF	Japanese Ground Self-Defense Force
JMSDF	Japanese Maritime Self-Defense Force
JSDF	Japanese Self-Defense Force
MLIT	Ministry of Land, Infrastructure, Transport and Tourism
MCDA	Military and Civil Defense Assets
MPAT	Multinational Planning Augmentation Tool
OCHA	Office for the Coordination of Humanitarian Affairs
OECD	Organization for Economic Cooperation and Development
OFDA	Office of Foreign Disaster Assistance
OHDACA	Overseas Humanitarian Disaster Assistance and Civic Aid
PACOM	U.S. Pacific Command
ROAP	Regional Office for Asia and the Pacific
TNI	Tentara Nasional Indonesia
USAID	United States Agency for International Development
USFJ	United States Forces Japan

THIS PAGE INTENTIONALLY LEFT BLANK

ACKNOWLEDGMENTS

I would like to thank my wife, Lara, for her continued faith through this process. Without her constant trust, I would likely have never been able to complete this paper. I would also endeavor to thank Professor Robert Weiner for his thoughtful perspective and engaging conversations over these past 18 months that have led to this thesis.

THIS PAGE INTENTIONALLY LEFT BLANK

I. INTRODUCTION

A. MAJOR RESEARCH QUESTION

Has the United States appropriately scaled its military maritime responses to humanitarian disasters within the Asia-Pacific region, more specifically, within the 2004 Aceh, Indonesia, disaster and within the response to the 2011 Great Japan Earthquake? Has the United States neglected to conduct accurate needs-based assessments and in turn responded to its regional partners with excess military capacity?

B. IMPORTANCE

The answer to this major research question is important for a number of reasons. As the United States continues to recognize the growing importance of Asia within the global community, a quantity of critical self-assessment is necessary as a preponderance of both military and diplomatic power shifts to the Pacific. Possessing an explicit policy of making its forces available for international humanitarian work, the United States military should be ever conscious in the application of its influence. Naval power remains especially viable as an agent for effective assistance yet military planners must remain cognizant of the scale of the respective response. The importance of this question is readily apparent on three different fronts.

First, U.S. military planners should strive to operate within accepted international standards and norms regarding the use of military forces and assets in support of humanitarian response to natural disasters. Robust international guidelines exist for this reason and the United States should continue its leadership in the Pacific in accordance with internationally accepted standards of behavior.

Second, the acceptance of humanitarian aid is never guaranteed and its assurance rests largely on perception and strong assessments of need. Consistency of response remains the greatest asset the U.S. military can wield within the Pacific as it continues to shape its perception to regional allies in Asia.[1]

Third and finally, U.S. military planners are beginning to accept the budgetary realities that will define capacity and employment even as resources shift into the Pacific. Successive Quadrennial Defense Review processes will likely continue to emphasize the importance of expeditionary forces. Future renditions of disaster relief efforts within the Pacific theater will provide military maritime planners the chance to utilize inherent flexibility and mobility within the fiscal restrictions of a future force.

C. PROBLEMS AND HYPOTHESES

This major research question raises a number of problems that I anticipate dealing with through the course of this work. First, I find it appropriate to enumerate the bounds of the question itself by acknowledging that I am by no means attempting to determine the efficacy of U.S. military response within disaster relief roles in the Pacific. I am not determining U.S. capability to impact the population of affected nations. Rather, I believe it is by fully understanding the potential for appropriately scaled levels of U.S. military assistance to disaster scenarios, military planners can find both more effective and appropriate responses that continue to reinforce the United States' role as a responsible partner within the Asia Pacific.

Second, first-hand experiences and second-hand accounting of personal interactions that detail the reluctance of affected nations accepting military assistance may prove difficult to correlate with larger, observable trends. Having had the opportunity to directly participate and assist within one of the aforementioned case studies, I feel the need to caveat this experience lest these singular interactions fail to manifest themselves upon a larger scale.

Based on existing literature, informant accounting, and observable trends, a number of preliminary conclusions can be made. Excess military capacity, be it in a bi-

---

[1] Steering Committee for Humanitarian Response, "Position Paper on Humanitarian-Military Relations, January 2010," accessed June 4, 2012, http://ochanet.unocha.org/p/Documents/Steering%20Committee%20for%20Humanitarian%20Response-%20SCHR%20position%20paper%20on%20humanitarian-military%20relations%20(2010).pdf

lateral theater security cooperation visit or a multi-lateral exercise, is often the standard when characterizing U.S. participation. This constancy combined with the forward-deployed nature of assets within Asia increases the likelihood that military capability will overwhelm affected nations. My primary hypothesis contends that the United States responded to the 2011 Japan Earthquake and Tsunami with maritime military capability that did not accurately reflect the needs of the host nation.

D.   LITERATURE REVIEW

1.   Introduction

The discussion of the role of the military during humanitarian disaster relief scenarios in Asia enjoys a large amount of literature due largely to successive disasters over the past decade. The majority document the effort to develop "collaborative guidelines to assist the planning of foreign military assistance" under the guise of the original 1994 "Oslo guidelines." These norms advocated by the United Nations Office for the Coordination of Humanitarian Affairs are the international community's attempt to force the internalization of the "core principles of humanity, neutrality, and impartiality" onto the military planning of partner nations.[2] The degree to which the United States has used this philosophy as its own, however, is under debate according to current literature. A report from the Stockholm International Peace Research Institute tracks a decade's worth of U.S. military intervention into the humanitarian realm as "not directly influenced by the Oslo guidelines." Instead, the United States claimed to base its "decisions on factors such as the ability to save lives, the feasibility of responding to specific requests and the availability of the requested assets and on decisions by governmental departments regarding deployment."[3]

In an effort to frame the importance of proficiency within civil relief institutions and the need for an effective and proficient military capability within states effected by humanitarian disasters, I wanted to briefly illuminate two additional case studies that I

---

[2] Sharon Wiharta et al., "The Effectiveness of Foreign Military assets in Natural Disaster Response," *Stockholm International Peace Research Institute*, 2008, 10.

[3] Ibid., 20.

will include within my thesis that I consider to be appropriate contextualized approaches to disaster relief. The February 2011 earthquake in Christchurch, New Zealand, killed over 185 people within the nation's second largest city, a disaster that would be certain to flex any response capability. Marshaling the assistance of nearly 500 international relief workers and rescue personnel, New Zealand implemented a full emergency management structure within two hours of the disasters, with national coordination wielded from the "National Crisis Management Centre bunker" in Wellington.[4] All told, this well-organized response to urban disaster was possible due to well-developed civil relief institutions despite the lack of what many in the international community would consider an overly effective military capability.

The second case that I feel necessary to mention and review in order to illuminate the importance of these two variables would be the earthquake in Haiti on 10 January 2010. The 7.0 magnitude quake, as well as a number of large aftershocks, severely damaged infrastructure within the Haitian capital of Port-au-Prince and created mass chaos within a country that already suffered from poor civil-military instructions. While the United States assumed a large role in organizing relief aid and logistics to the affected areas, the U.S. Navy provided a number of resources by deploying an entire Expeditionary Strike Group to the region. Lacking both civil-relief institutions and a capable military force, the robust Haitian relief effort was appropriate and necessary, yet striking in its size when compared to the greater number of assets responding to the 2011 Japan disaster.

Important within existing literature are any discrepancies that can further illuminate the ways in which the United States has either achieved or failed to pursue a "whole of government approach" toward disaster relief. A position paper from the Steering Committee for Humanitarian Response characterizes such a response as one that reinforces "the need to combine all means at a government's disposal—political, economic, military, developmental, and humanitarian assistance—to achieve

---

[4] "Christchurch Earthquake: Emergency Cabinet Meeting," *The Daily Post*, February 22, 2011, accessed August 23, 2012, http://www.rotoruadailypost.co.nz/news/christchurch-quake-emergency-cabinet-meeting/1045160/

stabilization."[5] With an eye for this type of balanced approach, the Center for Strategic and International Studies analyzed specific levels of funding from corporate and governmental organizations for both the 2004 Aceh disaster as well as the 2011 Japan earthquake and tsunami. As "the most rapidly and generously funded disaster assistance effort of all time," the 2004 event found the U.S. government soliciting funds from the likes of Pfizer, UNICEF, UPS, Coca-Cola and the UN Development program. The U.S. president solicited the assistance of his two predecessors in order to raise over $15 million in private funds. The same report documents stark contrasts within the 2011 Japan disaster. It was "demand rather than supply driven" and from the start, the "Japanese government has clearly articulated its need, requesting only minimal logistical and nuclear safety support." Companies such as Coca-Cola and Costco did assist but only by working in tandem with USAID to guarantee water supplies. Private companies had difficulty finding appropriate "entry points for action" in Japan while military planners encountered many of the same problems due to cumbersome "Japanese political and legal processes."[6] While the 2011 event in Japan lacked a disaster relief fund sponsored by the U.S. government, it seems interesting to reconcile that the U.S. military deployed assets in very comparable manners to both events.

2.   Affected Nation Absorptive Capacity and Appropriateness of Force

SIPRI uses both absorptive capacity and appropriateness of military assets as two of six interconnected factors that are useful in determining the efficacy of military assistance within a disaster relief scenario. The first speaks to the affected nation, specifically disaster management institutions, ability to coordinate and effectively use assets during a relief situation while the latter speaks to how will capabilities meet a need and how suitable such assets are for the local cultural and political context.[7] While efficacy itself is not in question for either of the two case studies examined, the factors

---

[5] "Position Paper on Humanitarian-Military Relations, January 2010," 3.

[6] Stacey White, "Corporate Engagement in Natural Disaster Response: Piecing Together the Value Chain," *Center for Strategic & International Studies*, January 2012, 16–20, accessed June 2, 2012, http://reliefweb.int/sites/reliefweb.int/files/resources/120117_White_CorporateEngagement_Web.pdf

[7] "The Effectiveness of Foreign Military Assets," xii.

above do assist in clarifying some of the initial findings I have found within current literature detailing the execution of each respective effort.

Of the literature that does currently discuss the 2011 Japan disaster, the majority caveats this effort as one that is abnormal and different. The Office for the Coordination of Humanitarian Affairs 2011 Annual Report is quite remarkable in that it commits literally one-half page to addressing the humanitarian efforts in the wake of Japan's earthquake and tsunami. In assuming a less-than-leading role in the effort, OCHA's 2011 report says, "Japan carefully selected the assistance it needed to support national response efforts." It documents that Japan "opted not to appeal for international assistance, despite offers of support from governments around the world."[8] A similar one-year report from the United Nations International Medical Corps applauds Japan's "significant disaster response capability" while documenting its stringent efforts to "partner" and "augment" existing institutions.[9]

The plaudits for Japan starkly contrast the critical reviews of Indonesian efforts during the 2004 disaster. SIPRI makes it clear that "Indonesia lacked an appropriate disaster response mechanism" and holds Bakornas as an institution that had neither assets, policy-making, nor enforcement powers. Early warning and disaster relief communication systems were nonexistent and provincial disaster management offices were woefully unprepared for any type of emergency. United Nations lessons learned held bureaucratic and institutional failings led to duplicative announcements with no clear understanding of roles and responsibilities. These failings, however, did not prevent Indonesia's government from opening Aceh to the humanitarian community and giving "almost free rein to aid organizations, and to expose itself to international scrutiny." The

---

[8] United Nations Office For the Coordination of Humanitarian Affairs, *Annual Report 2011*, 3, accessed June 2, 2012,
http://reliefweb.int/sites/reliefweb.int/files/resources/2011%20OCHA%20Annual%20Report%20Final%20150dpi.pdf

[9] International Medical Corps, *Japan: One Year Report*, 3, accessed June 2, 2012,
http://reliefweb.int/sites/reliefweb.int/files/resources/PDF_203.pdf

same report commends Indonesia for its liberal actions within the crises, and while its "ad hoc decisions" for such a laissez faire assistance policy "may not be ideal," they were certainly effective.[10]

E.   METHODS AND SOURCES

This academic study will adopt an inductive approach using qualitative analysis of two case studies, accompanied with data from a literature review and knowledge gathered from the interview of primary sources and informants. The 2004 Indian Ocean earthquake and tsunami as well as the March 2011 Great Japan earthquake and tsunami were chosen as just two of the many instances where the United States has employed military assets in a military capacity. These two studies in particular, however, are readily understood as complex, rapid-onset, and the most similar in severity within the Asia-Pacific. Within each the United States military provided direct assistance, aid that is defined by the United Nations as the "face-to-face distribution of goods and services."[11] Each complex disaster had immense impact on respective coastal, outlying communities while a comparative look at the two also provides diversity within the two intervening variables: the development of civil relief institutions and the organic military capabilities within the affected state.

The role of U.S. military assistance within the 2004 Indian Ocean disaster is well documented and enjoys nearly a decade of international discussion, assessment, and consensus. A great many academic endeavors employ the 2004 efforts as a definitive example of the effectiveness of military assistance in a humanitarian role. The unparalleled utilization of military forces following the 2004 disaster spurred the United Nations Office for the Coordination of Humanitarian Affairs Civil-Military Coordination Section to reexamine and update what are known within the international community as the "Oslo Accords"; a set of normative guidelines used to "provide improved coordination in the use of military and civil defence assets in response to natural,

---

[10] "The Effectiveness of Foreign Military Assets," 89–90.

[11] United Nations Office for the Coordination of Humanitarian Affairs, "Guidelines on The Use of Military and Civil Defence Assets in Disaster Relief—'Oslo Guidelines,'" Rev. 1, November 2006, 3.

technological and environmental emergencies in peacetime."[12]   This reassessment of international guidance in 2006 serves as a fitting backdrop against the unexamined scope of United States military response to the 2011 Great Japan earthquake and tsunami.

Counter to the documentation of U.S. efforts in the Indian Ocean, critical scholarship detailing the role of military assistance in Japan during the 2011 disaster remains largely anecdotal and collections of various open-source reporting from governmental agencies. I have been unable to find any literature critical of military movement, tasking, and mission and plan to collect information from a number of primary sources, both civilian and military, who will be able to contribute to this base of knowledge. Individual unit commanders, uniquely positioned staff members, as well as non-governmental organization employees who were present during all phases of relief efforts will provide detailed accounts of their perspectives, which I will use inductively to create observations on U.S. military actions within both respective disaster relief efforts.

An iterative progression of situation reports from such international aid organizations as the Japan Red Cross and the International Federation of Red Cross and Red Crescent Societies will provide accurate and timely data for each respective case study, as well as an understanding of the organic disaster relief capacity of each affected nation. The United Nation's Office for the Coordination of Humanitarian Affairs provides similarly detailed situational reports from each incident and provides an international perspective as well.

The examination of each affected nation's military capacity within the disaster relief realm will likely be challenging when examining the TNI's preparations for the 2004 Aceh disaster. Japan's Self Defense Forces provides relatively robust assessments of yearly actions through the Ministry of Defense while similar products are lacking from Indonesia with the notable exception of the Defence White Paper published in 2003.

---

[12] "The Effectiveness of Foreign Military Assets," 10.

8

F. THESIS OVERVIEW

The thesis will be structured through an examination of each of the two intervening variables within both the 2004 Aceh and 2011 Japan case studies. The second chapter will examine Humanitarian Disaster paradigms by defining accepted definitions, roles and responsibilities for nations who offer military assistance to disaster relief scenarios, as well as trends and patterns observed by USAID within Humanitarian Relief Operations within the Pacific over the previous decade. Both the third and fourth chapters will examine the ways in which the degree of civil relief institutions and organic military capabilities and effectiveness were accounted for within the military responses to both the 2004 Aceh Earthquake and Tsunami and the 2011 Japan Earthquake and Tsunami, respectively. I anticipate finding evidence of a failure to observe or understand either of these predictive variables which may indicate that military assistance was excessive in either one or both cases and it could have possible been avoided had military planners been cognizant of either of the dynamics. Upon completing this review, I will end the thesis with concluding remarks that will review key findings, examine prospects for fundamental change, as well as attempt to determine United States Security Policy Recommendations. I anticipate a number of areas of interest that merit further research, especially as additional supplementary analysis of the 2011 Japan Earthquake and Tsunami becomes available within the academic community.

THIS PAGE INTENTIONALLY LEFT BLANK

II. HUMANITARIAN DISASTER PARADIGMS

A. INTRODUCTION

In order to effectively gauge the possibility of excess military capacity in response to the humanitarian disasters of 2004 and 2011 in Indonesia and Japan, respectively, it is necessary to conduct a general discussion on the established norms and guidelines regarding the use of military assets to provide direct assistance. This chapter begins by examining the accepted guidelines as promulgated by the United Nation's Office for the Coordination of Humanitarian Affairs (OCHA), which will be followed by a discussion of six interconnected aspects of effectiveness in relation to the use of military assets in humanitarian roles across the world over the roughly previous fifteen years, and then finally a look at the United States Agency for International Development (USAID) and its guidance that dictates the ways in which civil authorities account for and accommodate military capabilities within humanitarian relief roles. Subsequently, I will conclude this chapter with a brief examination of two predictive variables that I deem to be most important in assessing need within disaster scenarios, the development of civil relief institutions and the organic military capabilities of an effected state, and then highlight those same variables within two minor case studies that illustrate their respective importance.

B. NORMS AND GUIDANCE

The role of the military in providing humanitarian assistance to civilians within foreign countries is not new and its future likelihood should not present any profound change in planning. Beginning in 1948 with the Berlin Airlift, military forces have been consistently involved with crises situations across the world. Regardless this fact, there are veins of institutional resistance that often times find it difficult to reconcile the inherently violent business of conveying physical force that military forces find themselves positioned to conduct. A study conducted by the Humanitarian Policy Group at the Overseas Development institute contests, however, that there are a few ways in which military forces and humanitarian efforts overlap.

First, there has been a long tradition of humanitarian concern within the conduct of war as seen within the *jus in bello* tradition that seeks to limit suffering caused within the conduct of military action. Such tradition "has shaped contemporary international humanitarian law, in particular the 1899 and 1907 Hague Conventions, the 1949 Geneva conventions and the 1977 Additional Protocols."[13] The various restrictions on cluster munitions, biological and chemical weapons, not to mention the recognition places on the role of the non-combatant reflect our need to serve humanitarian needs. Second, the *jus ad bello* tradition that in essence permits the conduct of war to serve humanitarian ends carries wide recognition through the history of international warfare. Seen at times as a moral impetus to intervene on behalf of an oppressed group or minority, such action cannot be seen as altogether different from providing humanitarian aid in the instance of such an oppressive event as complex natural disasters. Third and finally, the Humanitarian Policy Group illustrates what many recognize as the benefits of the military's organic capabilities of logistics, transport, and engineering within a humanitarian scenario. Rotary and fixed wing assets have served as force multipliers time and time again within any number of recent relief efforts and such military infrastructure can only continue to compliment humanitarian efforts in the future.[14]

1.   Oslo Guidelines and OCHA

Finalized within an international conference in Norway in January of 1994 and released four months later in May, the "Oslo Guidelines" reflected the collaborative efforts of over forty-five states and over one hundred and eighty delegates over a two-year process to encapsulate norms and guidance on the use of military assets within humanitarian assistance operations. The guidelines themselves have been promulgated since 1994 in an iterative fashion following the 2005 relief efforts in South East Asia and again in 2010. The coordinating body for this guidance remains the United Nations Office for the Coordination of Humanitarian Affairs (OCHA) and, at times more

---

[13] "Resetting the Rules of Engagement: Trends and Issues in Military-Humanitarian Relations," Humanitarian Policy Group at the Overseas Development Institute, 2006, 2.1, accessed June 2, 2012, http://ochanet.unocha.org/p/Documents/Humanitarian%20Policy%20Group%20Report%20Civil-Military%20Coordination.pdf

[14] Ibid., 2.1.

specifically, its Regional Office for Asia and the Pacific (ROAP) in Bangkok through the Asia-Pacific Military Assistance to Disaster Relief Operations series of Conferences (APC-MADRO), which are held annually within the region.[15]

Crucial to understanding the facets of the Oslo Guidelines is the necessity to delineate the ways in which the text defines assistance and those actors that can in certain instances provide relief aid. For the sake of these guidelines, assistance is divided into three categories based on the degree of contact with the affected population. Of these three categories, I will touch exclusively with the first two within the bounds of this paper due to the close interaction by assisting nation to the affected populace and the inherent perceptions generated by such personal assistance.

Direct assistance—the face-to-face distribution of goods and services

Infrastructure support—involves providing general services, such as road repair, airspace management and power generation that facilitate relief, but are not necessarily visible to or solely for the benefit of the affected population

Indirect Assistance—at least one step removed from the population and involves such activities as transporting relief goods or relief personnel.[16]

Directly facilitating assistance through any of the three avenues depicted above, the guidelines define International Disaster Relief Assistance (IDRA) to include "material, personnel and services provided by the international community to an Affected State to meet the needs of those affected by a disaster." The 2006 version of the guidelines continues to define the totality of military assistance within a disaster scenario as Military and Civil Defense Assets (MCDA), a description which includes all "relief personnel, equipment, supplies and services provided by foreign military and civil defense organizations for IDRA."[17]

---

[15] United Nations Office for the Coordination of Humanitarian Affairs, "Guidelines on the Use of Military and Civil Defence Assets in Disaster Relief—'Oslo Guidelines,'" Rev. 1, November 2006, 1.

[16] "Guidelines on the Use of Military and Civil Defence Assets," 3.

[17] Ibid., 3.

Within the Oslo Guidelines, any movement toward providing humanitarian assistance must be facilitated in accordance with the core principles of humanity, neutrality, and impartiality as well as in conjunction with a full respect for "the sovereignty, territorial integrity and national unity of States."[18] The numerous references of the necessity to coordinate with and provide relief at the consent of the Affected nation throughout the non-binding Oslo Guidelines bookends well with the declarations of non-interference found throughout the Asia-Pacific region and ASEAN nations and is a principle that must be well-understood by any Assisting nations that undertake to provide MCDA. In addition, the Assisting nation within a disaster relief scenario is tasked with seeking "initial and on-going assessments from the appropriate coordinating body" endeavor to share such assessments of need with other actors involved in the relief. Similarly, military response to any Requests for Assistance (RFA) should be coordinated in such a manner to "minimize duplication, confusion, and gaps in support."[19] Finally, a key tenet dictating the use of foreign military assets within the IDRA is the concept of "last resort"; this principle asserts that such capabilities will be utilized when "there is no comparable civilian alternative" available at the time and location needed and such military capability can only be used when meeting a "critical humanitarian need."[20]

Moreover, the emphasis placed on providing "complimentary relief" is perhaps the most important concept for the United States and other more capable militaries to grasp. The necessity for nations to coordinate their relief efforts with the effected nation, or in essence, be seen as a force motivated toward extending existing relief mechanisms in response to a mutually acknowledged "humanitarian gap" between the disaster needs that the relief community is being asked to satisfy and the resources available to meet them.[21] Understanding as much further illustrates the importance of considering the

---

[18] Ibid., 7.

[19] "Asia-Pacific Regional Guidelines For the Use of Foreign Military Assets in Natural Disaster Response Operations," DRAFT Version 8.0, November 23, 2010, 11. Working paper developed through Asia-Pacific Military Assistance to Disaster Relief Operations series of conferences.

[20] "Asia-Pacific Regional Guidelines," 5.

[21] Guidelines On the use of Military and Civil Defense Assets, 7.

intervening variables of the development of civil relief institutions and the organic military capabilities within the affected state prior to the assumption of humanitarian response activities by outside nations.

2.   Observed Trends and Practices

Understanding the strict confines within which United Nations forces must adhere while participating within humanitarian relief operations, the Oslo Guidelines do their best to dictate the terms and circumstances for the deployment of UN MCDA within an affected nation. Acknowledging, however, that United Nations military capabilities are rarely utilized for sudden onset disasters, the Oslo guidelines themselves must be acknowledged as a point of departure for other nations to utilize in their humanitarian responses. A thorough study by the Stockholm International Peace Research Institute (SIPRI) conducted in 2008 that was supported by OCHA attempted to determine the real-world advantages, limitations, and implications of utilizing foreign military assets in response to natural disasters. The study undertook to examine the deployments of military units through the proceeding eleven years and explicitly concedes that rarely do requests for assistance find themselves at the UN OCHA offices. Rather, the study opens by asserting that "most deployments of foreign military assets in disaster relief come through direct, bilateral negotiations between governments, or even between national militaries, based on established relationships."[22]   Continuing, the study indicates that included within the 1997–2006 purview of examination, the United States consistently deployed its military assets "most frequently and in the greatest volume—15 times between 2003 and 2006 for disaster relief."[23]   Noting that often times despite the normative framework provided by the Oslo Guidelines, the application of such behavior remains uneven across the national level. It was with this understanding that scholars at SIPRI developed six interconnected aspects of effectiveness in the use of foreign military assets: timeliness, appropriateness, efficiency, absorptive capacity, coordination, and

---

[22] Sharon Wiharta et al., "The Effectiveness of Foreign Military Assets in Natural Disaster Response," *Stockholm International Peace Research Institute*, 2008, xi.

[23] "The Effectiveness of Foreign Military Assets," x.

costs.[24] These six aspects of effective relief were chosen due because they were either deemed operationally pertinent to real-world scenarios, or they were considered pertinent to the established Oslo Guidelines as well as the Organization for Economic Cooperation and Development (OECD) Development Assistance Committee evaluation requirements.[25] Not intending one singular factor to be more prominent or important that any other, SIPRI thought these six served best as a starting point for developing tools of critical analysis to make the important decision to utilize military assets within a disaster scenario.

(1)   Timeliness. The needs within a humanitarian relief operation upon the sudden onset of devastation are quite unique and often are time-critical in a matter of hours. It is with this consideration of the surge phase of a scenario that often dictates the necessity of a military response due to an armed force's ability to quickly marshal assets and supplies in a manner befitting the crises. Throughout all of the case studies examined by SIPRI within the eleven-year period, "neighboring countries and regional actors were generally the first to be approached for assistance and also the first to deploy military assets."[26] The efficacy of military units in such a scenario should be gauged by the speed of their deployment relative to civilian assets with the same capabilities, if such assets are to be found in the region. I personally hold the timeliness gauge of efficacy to be a difficult one due to the delicate balance between the deployment of likely nearby military assets and the need for accurate initial needs assessment. Provided a lack of reliable information regarding the scale and complexity of a disaster, or reports erring in their overestimation of the disaster altogether, the relief efforts of military assets in close proximity to a disaster may in turn be less efficient due to their initial responses.

(2)   Appropriateness. SIPRI finds that often times any discussion of appropriateness within the use of military assets in disaster relief falls along two lines: first, a question of whether the assets provided are appropriate for a specific

---

[24] Ibid., 31

[25] Ibid., 31.

[26] Ibid., 32.

task and second, within which scenarios is it appropriate to substitute military capabilities for civilian ones within disaster relief, a discussion which relates back to the Oslo Guidelines principles of "last resort."[27] The first question has clear implications in that improperly suited tools will likely perform badly if at all within a context that does not call for their use and military planners run the risk of complicating or cluttering an already complex environment by supplying military assets inappropriate to the task at hand. The risk of such an occasion can be reduced with continued emphasis on a continuing needs based assessment process that should further shape and refine needs as disaster scenarios progress. In dealing with the second of the two questions raised by the scholars, that which questions the appropriate use of military assets within the context of humanitarian relief, further illuminates the need to be cognizant of both deployment lengths and possible perceptions of such use from the host nation on both national and individual levels. Clearly understanding the need to withdraw forces "while they're still waving at you with all five fingers" remains a challenge for military planners today as does differentiating between the reactions our relief efforts may spur from local residents and government officials, as well as such instances when the reactions differ.[28]

(3) Efficiency. The examination of efficiency within this context by SIPRI references whether military assets are operation efficiently as stand-alone assets as well as to whether they are competently employed within the overall effort. Be it aviation flight hours of helicopter squadrons, payload sling capacities, or burn rates or marine diesel fuel, each can prove vitally important to maximizing the full spectrum of resources available to military planners within a disaster relief operation. The authors of this study also point to the understood notion that military units are designed to operate as stand-alone entities which often entails the inclusion of various maintenance redundancies of equipment and personnel that will likely necessitate a larger footprint. Once again, the value of an initial accurate need based assessment drives a number of the factors included herein and efficiency almost more than any other.

(4) Absorptive Capacity

---

[27] Ibid., 34–35.

[28] Ibid., 37.

An affected nation's absorptive capacity indicates the ability of such a nation to effectively facilitate and coordinate foreign military assets during a disaster relief scenario. Whether it be existing civil relief organizations or impromptu relief infrastructures, aiding nations are bound to utilize existing structures in order to complement and tailor their relief efforts. Put succinctly, "strong governments are generally in a better position to take responsibility for relief efforts that weaker ones."[29] Efficient domestic institutions within the affected state should prove positive indicators for effective coordination and accurate assessments of need. Military planners should expect the opposite to hold true as well; if an affected nation's civil relief institutions are weak to non-existent, supporting international partners will likely find themselves left with the responsibility of coordinating and effecting the relief largely on their own accord. Finally, military planners responding to disaster scenarios within affected nations with strong and established relief mechanisms should do so with a measured sense of respect and understanding lest such strong countries harbor institutional resistances toward accepting foreign assistance.

(5)   Coordination. This aspect of effectiveness in the use of foreign military assets within disaster relief roles lends itself largely toward an understanding and emphasis on communicating across the wide range of actors that surge together within the opening phases of any humanitarian relief operation. Understanding that coordination is often most lacking within the first few days of any response, effective strategies for conducting civil-military coordination can alleviate much of friction encountered when military units assume their role within the area. Carrying out joint needs assessments is one of the initial steps recommended by SIPRI in bridging this civil-military gulf, as well as the benefits seen from establishing institutional relationships with information sharing and liaison officers. Similarly, established relationship between host nation and assisting militaries can at times enhance inter-operability and trust within humanitarian relief efforts.[30] Increased bi-lateral engagement should be seen as a "dress rehearsal" of sorts for any future contingency operations.

---

[29] Ibid., 39.

[30] Ibid., 42.

18

(6)   Costs

Sixth and finally, considerations of costs are often passionately discussed in regards to humanitarian relief operations. Oslo Guidelines succinctly posit that military relief should be offered at no cost to the affected nation barring any prior agreement to the contrary.[31] The question then often becomes, can the deployment of military assets by a particular nation be covered within humanitarian aid budgets rather than those for general defense? The authors of this study remark that they have seen a wide range of approaches from various countries through the eleven years of disasters yet the most common either hold the defense budgetary processes responsible for the entire amount or nations split the costs between defense and humanitarian requisitions, respectively. In such instances, where deployment costs are borne entirely by pre-existing defense lines of accounting, military responses to disasters "become a highly cost-effective option." Often times, humanitarian budgetary processes are incidental to each particular disaster and can prove time consuming and laborious to implement.[32]

3.   U.S. Military Trends and Practices within Disaster Relief

In exploring the normative behavior associated with the use of military assets within disaster relief scenarios, I have touched upon the 1994 "Oslo Guidelines" as well as the established trends and patterns that followed in the decade after its dissemination to United Nations members. I will now specifically address the regulations and requirements for the use and coordination of United States military capabilities within international disaster situations. There is one key facet for U.S. military planners to remember within this context; the Department of Defense (DoD) plays a supporting role

---

[31] Ibid., 43.

[32] Ibid., 45.

within these types of operations. In short, the U.S. Ambassador within an affected country sets policy and directs the U.S. government team, while the U.S. Agency for International Development (USAID) and within it, the Office of Foreign Disaster Assistance (OFDA), coordinate and manage the U.S. response.[33] I will continue this section by touch on the steps necessary to initiate a U.S. government response to an international humanitarian disaster, to include the U.S. military, as well as discuss a number of the dynamics pertinent to military planners operating in such a scenario.

There are three main criteria that must be met in order for a U.S. Ambassador or Chief of Mission (COM) to declare a disaster: the situation exceeds the host nation's ability to respond; the affected country's government either requests or is willing to receive U.S. assistance; and a response to the disaster is within the U.S. national interest.[34] Such an assertion is sent to the OFDA and Department of State (DoS) in Washington, DC, in order to begin a whole of government response. Figure 1 details much of the same:

---

[33] Cathal O'Connor, "Foreign Humanitarian Assistance and Disaster-Relief Operations: Lessons Learned and Best Practices," *Naval War College Review*, Winter 2012, Vol. 65, No. 1, 1.

[34] "Foreign Humanitarian Assistance," Joint Publication 3–29, U.S. Defense Department, Washington D.C., March 17, 2009, II-4.

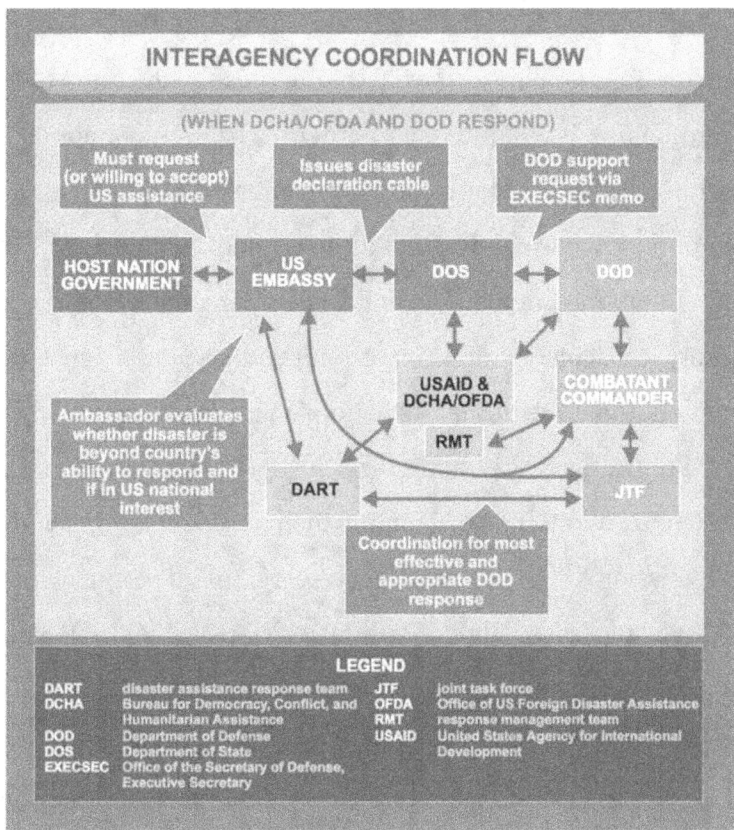

Figure 1.   Interagency Coordination Flow (From Joint Publication 3–29, 2009).[35]

The OFDA will in most instances deploy a Disaster Assistance Response Team (DART) to the affected nation in order to begin coordination the humanitarian relief effort. Such a team will include specialists and subject matter experts specific to each scenario that are tasked with liaising with U.S. embassies and other governmental organizations, such as the U.S. military, that may be involved in the effort.[36] Within the DoD itself, the Assistant Secretary for Defense for Global Security Affairs is responsible for foreign disaster assistance policy as well as a number of fiscal obligations that are inherent in coordinating such a mission across departmental lines.[37]

Key within the opening phase of any U.S. military response to a disaster scenario is the action of the Humanitarian Assistance Survey Team (HAST) as tasked by

---

[35] Cathal O'Connor, "Foreign Humanitarian Assistance," II-6.

[36] Ibid., 11–6

[37] Ibid., 11–7.

its respective military Combatant Commander. Assigned the responsibility to begin gathering information for planning, a HAST should liaise with country teams and USAID representatives through the U.S. Embassy in order to determine a number of things. Such important initial observations include: primary points of contact; the capability of the Host Nation government to respond to the disaster; and formulate recommendations for provision of DoD funding, equipment, supplies, and personnel.[38] One of the underlying dynamics of military assistance within foreign humanitarian assistance (FHA) operations is the constant reminder that the military's actions must complement ongoing civilian and HN efforts. Joint Publication 3–29 addresses this specifically when it states, "military commanders must be cautious not to commit their forces to projects and tasks that go beyond the FHA mission."[39] This statement serves as a pertinent counter-point to a cautiously predictive statement found within USAID's Field Operations Guide for Disaster Assistance and Response, including added emphasis that was not my own. In attempting to explain the military's organizational culture to a likely civilian USAID DART member, the Field Operations Guide stresses the need for coordinated operations by emphasizing the need for "interagency coordination and a single focus. **Bereft of outside agency input, the military will generally fill a void as it sees fit**."[40] Violating this tenet has fiscal implications that are all too common and necessary to comprehend within this climate of fiscal austerity.

a.   OHDACA Considerations

Moving the spectrum of military operations beyond that of an FHA mission has consequences that jeopardize the delicate appropriation of Overseas Humanitarian Disaster Assistance and Civic Aid (OHDACA) funds. These monies are intended for the implementation of "low cost, non-obtrusive but highly effective activities that help partners help themselves, improves access to areas not otherwise available to

---

[38] Ibid., 11–9.

[39] Ibid., xi.

[40] "Field Operations Guide for Disaster Assessment and Response," U.S. Agency for International Development, Version 4.0, September 2005, F-6, accessed October 9, 2012. http://transition.usaid.gov/our_work/humanitarian_assistance/disaster_assistance/resources/pdf/fog_v4.pdf.

U.S. Forces, and build collaborative relationships."[41] At the disposal of the Secretary of Defense and his Combatant Commanders, these funds can be utilized under three umbrellas: humanitarian assistance (HA) programs; the humanitarian mine action (HMA) program; and within foreign disaster relief initiatives. In regards to the third and most pertinent of these funding justifications, the Defense Security Cooperation Agency (DSCA) notes the fact that the U.S. military offers attractive "stopgap" measures that are often critical within the early stages of a crises and can be utilized within an emergency response capacity. Put more clearly, "emergency response" is defined in this instance by the DSCA as action involving the support and delivery of emergency rations, "search and rescue, medical evacuation, and assistance to internally displaced persons and refugees."[42] Military operations within a disaster scenario falling outside of the bounds of these would therefore not be covered by OHDACA funding and would likely be beyond the scope of the FHA operation. The U.S. military's duty regarding emergency responses within the opening stages of a crisis are further delineated within Joint Publication 3–29 within the context of "immediate response." Accordingly, a commander may undertake such action "when time is of the essence to prevent human suffering and loss of life." While reimbursement of such immediate actions is not guaranteed, military units are explicitly advised to avoid "mission creep" amidst the comprehension that as the disaster scenario continues to develop, the "less likely that the assistance will be deemed immediate response."[43]

4.   Predictive Variables within FHA Assessments

As previously discussed in detail, the consequences of exceeding the restrictions placed on the actions of military assets within disaster relief operations are indeed real and carry concrete fiscal if not literal consequences within a complex scenario. While the

---

[41] "Fiscal Year 2011 Budget Estimates: Overseas Humanitarian, Disaster Assistance, and Civic Aid." Ppt available online from the Defense Security Cooperation Agency, Defense Security Cooperation Agency, 3.
http://comptroller.defense.gov/defbudget/fy2011/budet_justification/pdfs/01_Operation_and_Maintenance/ O_M_VOL_1_PARTS/OHDACA_FY11.pdf Accessed September 11, 2012.

[42] "Fiscal Year 2011 Budget Estimates," 9.

[43] "Foreign Humanitarian Assistance," B-3.

Oslo Guidelines and current U.S. policy as promulgated through joint publications and policy statements present a "best case" example, the six observed aspects of effectiveness supplied by SIPRI speak the difficulty of achieving exceptional scenarios. While this friction could in some case be attributed to the real-world dynamics of incalculably devastating scenarios, I believe that an underlying failure to understand the operational environment of disaster scenarios lies at the heart of unintended failures to supply military aid efficiently. Termed within the military as the process of joint intelligence preparation of the operational environment (JIPOE), this necessary function within rapid onset and complex disaster relief scenarios requires a degree of foresight within each unique operational theater. It was noted previously that the presence of pre-existing relief agencies and institutions within disaster regions could drastically affect the way foreign military assistance is received and facilitated within a host nation. Joint Publication 3–29 acknowledges the challenges inherent within adapting the military's JIPOE process toward FHA operations, a task that requires a "different mindset and different techniques" altogether dissimilar from defeating an enemy with violent force.[44] The military's joint publication on operating within FHA scenarios continues the JIPOE discussion by offering up to seventeen diverse and unique "assessment factors" that range from cultural, sociological, and economic indicators that could prove useful to the assessment and planning process.[45] I argue, however, that there are two uniquely important predictive variables that yield the greatest degree of assessment value within JIPOE within a FHA scenario. Furthermore, I intend to argue through the examination of two recent and similarly severe case studies that U.S. military planners failed to fully recognize these two indicators in their assessment and conduct rendering aid to Japan after the March, 2011 earthquake and tsunami.

---

[44] Ibid., III-6.

[45] Ibid., III-7.

a. *Development of Civil Relief Institutions*

The presence of efficient and established conduits for relief within a given host nation should provide some degree of comfort and reliability to an assisting foreign military within a disaster relief scenario, as well as instill attitudes of respect and openness in light of this observed competence. Ranging from International Red Crescent / Red Cross organizations to albeit bureaucratic but efficient governmental ministries, proficient civil relief institutions should organically possess ample sources of funding, international recognition and credibility, as well as a history of functioning well under previous crises scenarios. An understood lack of corruption, as well as an ability to marshal the resources of the host nation's private sector, are also positive indicators of a competent and reliable civil relief institution that may very well serve as an able partner for foreign militaries within FHA operations.

b. *Organic Military Capabilities*

Similar to competent civil relief institutions, proficient host nation militaries can serve as a "trusted agent" to assisting foreign militaries within disaster relief situations. Possessing an operational familiarity that can prove invaluable, organic military capabilities have the ability to engage and assist host nation nationals that foreign militaries do not. Similarly, if the existing military structures within a disaster zone are deficient in resources, capability, and even a trusted role within society, foreign nations rendering aid may expect to offer a larger spectrum of service and support. As military planners seek to provide services within these situations that are both complementary and unburdening, a full understanding of our partner military's roles within society and its respective proficiency at wielding instrumental change is vitally important.

C. CONCLUSION

This chapter sought to begin the discussion of general trends and patterns within the utilization of military assets in humanitarian disaster scenarios. The Oslo Guidelines as promulgated through OCHA and United Nations partners establish a noticeably non-binding set of norms that have been adopted to a large degree across the international community since its release in 1994. Furthermore, the Stockholm International Peace Research Institute undertook an examination of military deployments in support of humanitarian causes across the decade following the Oslo Guidelines' release. The six observed aspects of effectiveness as seen through a variety of real-world scenarios were found to be: timeliness, appropriateness, efficiency, absorptive capacity, coordination, and costs. Turning toward specific U.S. guidance on the topic, the Department of Defense can expect to play a supporting role within a larger government approach led by the Department of State and in turn, USAID and OFDA. In order to emphasize the vital necessity for inter-agency coordination within the opening phases of any humanitarian response, a number of military joint publications and civilian policy documents cautiously cite the risk in allowing military commanders to exceed the bounds of their compassionate mission. Finally, I asserted that military planners within FHA roles can often gauge indicators of success or effectiveness based off of two predictive variables; the development of civil relief institutions and organic military capabilities within the affected state. I hold that military planners feigned ignorance to these variables within their response to the 2011 earthquake and tsunami in Japan and I intend to utilize two case studies to explore my argument.

III. JAPAN EARTHQUAKE AND TSUNAMI (2011)

A. INTRODUCTION

On March 11, 2011, a magnitude 9.0 earthquake struck approximately eighty miles east of Japan and two hundred and thirty miles northeast of Tokyo, prompting a successive wave of tsunamis to strike the country's largest island, Honshu. Impacting for four million homes across northern Japan, this devastation combination of natural events led to what many have since declared to be the most expensive natural disaster to date. Within this chapter, I will touch on the scope and severity of this event, as well as subsequent actions undertaken by U.S. forces forward deployed to the country prior to the disaster. While the movements of large military assets have been well covered by open-source media reporting since this event occurred last year, it is the interplay and coordination between DoD assets and USAID OFDA officials that I hope to discuss. Following this I will raise a number of points that I believe indicate a relative degree of competence within Japan's civil relief institutions as well as its Self Defense Forces.

B. SCOPE OF THE DISASTER

Marking what the United Nation's Office for the Coordination of Humanitarian Affairs referred to as the deadliest disaster of 2011 with nearly 20,000 dead and around $210 billion in damages, the Tohoku earthquake and tsunami was a massive event that drew immediate support both from the international community and within the Asia-Pacific region.[46] Measured on its metrics alone, the 9.0 magnitude earthquake would rank as the world's fourth largest since the year 1900 and would through its occurrence shift the seafloor nearly eighty feet westwards above the quake center, moving Honshu roughly 8 feet closer to California, and also shift the Earth on its axis by four inches.[47] Within half an hour of the first reports of an earthquake, tsunami floodwaters reached

---

[46] "OCHA 2011 Annual Report," Office for the Coordination of Humanitarian Affairs, May 2012, 3, accessed on August 2, 2012. www.unocha.org/annualreport/2011.

[47] Kevin Voigt, "Quake Moved Japan Coast 8 feet, Shifted Earth's Axis," *CNN*, April 20 2011, accessed September 4, 2012, http://www.cnn.com/2011/WORLD/asiapcf/03/12/japan.earthquake.tsunami.earth/index.html.

nearly six miles inland in some instances and instantly triggered similar tsunami warnings in over fifty countries in nations as far away as Chile, Canada, and the west coast of the United States. Over one hundred and sixty aftershocks, one hundred and forty one of which registered over a magnitude of 5.0, struck the area within the first twenty-four hours following the quake.[48] Within the most heavily affected prefectures, Fukushima, Miyagi, and Iwate, approximately 75,215 persons were displaced into evacuation centers or various other forms of temporary housing.[49] Due in part to the heavy concentration of the populace along coastal regions of northern Honshu, "over 432,047 homes and 27, 019 other buildings, as well as 3,700 roads were either damaged or destroyed completely."[50]

C.   U.S. RESPONSE

Within this section I will be detailing the actions undertaken by U.S. maritime forces within the disaster relief response to the March 11 earthquake and tsunami in Japan. By discussing the utilization of nearly 15,000 Marines and Sailors over a three-week period while also highlighting instances of ill-suited and excess capacity, I intend to illustrate the excessive nature of the U.S. naval response to this humanitarian disaster. Subsequent data as taken from USAID OFDA evaluating processes will further reinforce this perspective by condensing Japan's actual requests for foreign military assistance into an easily understood format.

The infrastructure provided by forward deployed U.S. forces in Japan as well as transiting assets within the Pacific region facilitated a rapid U.S. response to the events on March 11th. Commander U.S. Pacific Command (PACOM) tasked the Commander of U.S. Forces Japan (USFJ) as the Operational Supported Commander for Operation Tomodachi. Functional Component Commanders were further delineated within a 15 March task organizational message and are indicated in Figure 2.

---

[48] Ibid.

[49] "Japan: Earthquake and Tsunami Operations Update No. 4," Japanese Red Cross Society, June 29 2011, accessed June 2, 2012. http://reliefweb.int/report/japan/earthquake-and-tsunami-operations-update-n°-4

[50] Andrew Feickert and Emma Chanlett-Avery, "Japan 2011 Earthquake: U.S. Department of Defense (DoD) Response," *Congressional Research Service*, June 2, 2011, 1.

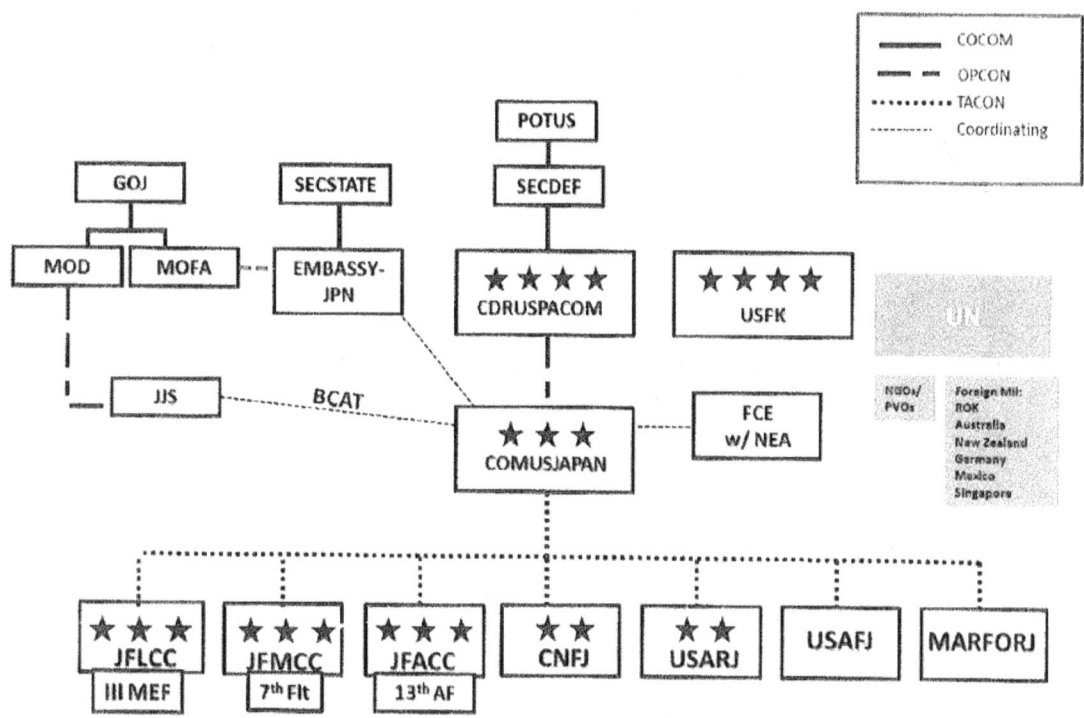

Figure 2.   Operation Tomodachi Task Organization (From USFJ TASKORD 1 to
OPORD 11–01 150845ZMAR11)

As stated, the mission for all forces in receipt of this U.S. Forces Japan tasking order was to "conduct HA/DR operations in support of the government of Japan and Japanese Self-Defense Forces efforts in Japan to alleviate human suffering and accelerate relief efforts until such time as the government of Japan no longer requires HA/DR assistance."[51] As mentioned previously in Chapter II, the necessity to define the timeline for the delivery of "immediate relief" is legitimate and USFJ addresses this as well when it states, "while lives are in danger and commanders are in a position to render life-saving assistance, commanders may provide such support using organic assets."[52]

After designating the Joint Forces Maritime Component Commander (JFMCC) as U.S. 7th Fleet, stationed in Yokosuka, Japan the U.S. Forces Japan TASKORD further

---

[51] U.S. Forces Japan Task Organization Message to Operational Order 11–01, Date Time Group 150845ZMAR11

[52] U.S. Forces Japan Task Organization Message to Operational Order 11–01, Date Time Group 150845ZMAR11

delineated a number of tasks to the maritime component commander in support of this disaster operation. Such specified tasks included:

- SAR element for surrounding sea areas of Japan supporting Joint Forces Air Component Commander (JFACC)

- Support Japanese Maritime Self Defense Force (JMSDF) humanitarian response

- Support USFJ J2 in disaster assessment and surveillance

- Support government of Japan (GoJ) in movement of disaster responders across the maritime environment

- Support JFACC in airspace management

- Be prepared to (BPT) accept and control airspace in the maritime environment

- Provide Maritime Response Cell (MRC) to USFJ

- BPT coordinate across the functional components

- Report capability shortfalls and accompany thing mitigation to USFJ

- Provide planner to USFJ J52 Planning Cell

- Coordinate and liaise with JMSDF

- Send SITREPs daily NLT 0500 and 1700 JST[53]

In marshaling support for relief efforts, U.S. 7th Fleet provided, by far, the largest continent of U.S. service members within Operation Tomodachi. Over 15,000 thousand Sailors and Marines participated within the JFMCC response over the roughly three weeks after March 11th, to include the approximately 2,200 Marines within the 31st Marine Expeditionary Unit (MEU) aboard Expeditionary Strike Group 7 (ESG-7) ships.[54] The USS *Ronald Reagan* Carrier Strike Group (CSG), which had been previously transiting through the 7th Fleet Area of Responsibility (AOR) after naval exercises with the Republic of Korea, was one of the first naval units to respond, in addition to its accompanying escorts. Forward deployed assets within Yokosuka further increased the number of U.S. assets responding, as did the presence of the USS *ESSEX*

---

[53] Ibid.

[54] U.S. Forces Japan Powerpoint Presentation entitled "Japan-U.S.-ROK CIV-MIL Disaster Preparedness Workshop, 29 September 2011, U.S. Embassy, Tokyo." Received from Mr. Daren Epstein, USFJ Deputy Director, Strategic Plans and Policy on September 5, 2012.

ESG with the 31st MEU embarked. A complete list of responding JFMCC forces is listed below:

- C7F on USS BLUE RIDGE
- RRN CSG, CVW-14, 2 CRUDES
- ESSEX ARG/31st MEU (4 ships)
- 7 x FDNF CRUDES
- 6 x CLF ships and USNS SAFEGUARD
- 2 x P-3, 2 x MH-53, 14 X H60[55]

The cruiser and destroyer (CRUDES) ships responding to the crises escorted the RRN, conducted search and rescue missions that began on March 13th, as well as flew hundreds of sorties to deliver humanitarian supplies to the affected areas.[56] Key to the speed of these operations was the established strength of the bond between the U.S. Navy and the JMSDF. Exchanging liaison officers and coordinating relief missions into affected areas, the USN and JMSDF team was even requested to cease operations at one point by the Joint Task Force at USFJ so as to allow for a "re-baseline" amongst components.[57] Absent, however, was any coordination between military units rendering rescue supplies to areas of northern Japan and USAID DART representatives within the USFJ bilateral command center.

USS *TORTUGA* assisted the Japanese Ground Self Defense Force (JGSDF) by moving nearly 100 vehicles and 300 SDF personnel from Hokkaido to northern Honshu and thus facilitated faster relief. Subsequently, *TORTUGA* became the flagship for Task Group 776.36, a port clearance group that consisted of USNS SAFEGUARD, 2 x MH-53, an Explosive Ordinance Disposal (EOD) platoon, as well as a Mobile Diving and Salvage Unit (MDSU) company. Tasked with assisting Japanese ports along north east Honshu with clearing a number of containers, vessels, and other debris blocking access to vital pier space, the port clearance unit assisted the Japanese suggested ports of

---

[55] Ibid.

[56] Andrew Feickert and Emma Chanlett-Avery, "Japan 2011 Earthquake," 6.

[57] Cathal O'Connor, "Foreign Humanitarian Assistance," 159.

Hachinohe Ko, Miyako Ko, and Kesennuma Ko between March 24th and April 8th.[58] Most notably, of the three ports assisted, two had already begun significant clearance operations and local officials within Miyako even requested the group not to conduct salvage operations "because they would prefer for local salvage experts" to clear the port.[59]

Within many of the immediate summaries detailing the participation of individual units within Operation Tomodachi, the 31st MEU is noticeably absent. It was not until April 1st that 187 Sailors and Marines from ESSEX went ashore on the remote island of Oshima under the auspices of Operation Field Day, an operation that was in reality a community relations project that lacked a host nation demand signal.[60]

1.   Coordination with USAID

In an effort to validate requests for assistance from the government of Japan as well as validate necessary requirements for the allocation of the previously mentioned OHDACA funding, U.S. Forces Japan disseminated a message on March 19th detailing the formation of a daily Joint Requirement Review Board (JRRB). Citing the requirement to "validate requirements, develop requirement prioritization," as well as determine the best method to meet host nation requests, at requirements were to be submitted through the JRRB with a completed USAID Mission Tasking Matrix (MITAM). Stated clearly within the USFJ message, "failure to obtain JRRB approval prior to obligation of funds for Operation Tomodachi in support of all lines of operations puts reimbursement of those service funds at risk," thereby implying that missions not appropriately sourced and approved with a completed MITAM would not be funded with OHDACA funds and additionally be found to be not immediately pertinent to disaster relief efforts.[61] USAID's FY2012 DHCA/OFDA Policy Cable even further illuminates the need for the

---

[58] Port Clearance Group Powerpoint Presentation entitled "CTG 776.63—Salvage and Recovery Force Operation TOMODACHI," received from CAPT Thomas Shaw on April 4, 2012.

[59] "Chronology of Operation Tomodachi," The National Bureau of Asian Research, accessed September 3, 2012. http://www.nbr.org/research/activity.aspx?id=121

[60] Ibid.

[61] U.S. Forces Japan message establishing a Joint Requirement Review Board, Date Time Group 192341ZMAR11.

MITAM process within a DoD operational planning cycle, stating that the sequence "generally validates and prioritizes DoD missions." At a minimum, all DoD disaster response activities, "including small projects," should be coordinated through OFDA even with the Department of State or OFDA do not make specific requests for assistance.[62]

All told, nearly 24,000 U.S. personnel, 189 aircraft, and 24 ships responded to the call for assistance within Operation Tomodachi yet the Joint Requirement Review Board facilitated by USFJ and OFDA processed merely 48 requests for support.[63] The 48 MITAMS were filed over a period of 15 March through 5 April. Only 29 of these 48 originated from the government of Japan and its subsequent organizations. The nature of these MITAMs is detailed in Figure 3.

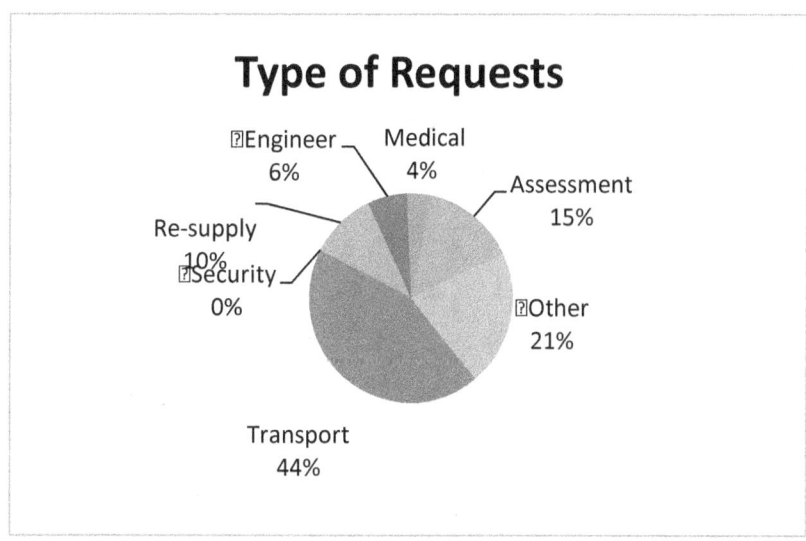

Figure 3.   MITAM Data from Operation Tomodachi (From USAID OFDA DART Lead, 09/20/2012).

Notably absent from the 48 requested missions for the U.S. military is a 6-day community relations project for the U.S. Marine Corps.[64]

---

[62] "FY2012 DCHA/OFDA Policy Cable Containing Guidance on Disaster Planning Response," United States Agency for International Development, February 13, 2012, 12, accessed October 2, 2012, http://transition.usaid.gov/policy/ads/200/251mad.pdf

[63] Andrew Feickert and Emma Chanlett-Avery, "Japan 2011 Earthquake," 1.

[64] MITAM Data received from USAID OFDA DART Lead, 09/20/2012.

D. PREDICTIVE VARIABLES

As discussed previously in Chapter II, I hold two predictive variables as most important for military planners as they attempt to understand the operational space prior to providing humanitarian relief in a foreign nation. I will now briefly touch on the proficiency and capabilities of Japan's organic civil relief and aid institution as well as the country's own military ability to respond to a natural disaster.

1. Civil Relief Institutions

Japan possesses a robust response to domestic humanitarian disasters, within both civil bureaucratic ministries and aid relief organizations. The United Nation's Office for the Coordination of Humanitarian Affairs 2011 Annual Report commends the Humanitarian Assistance and Emergency Relief Division within the Ministry of Foreign Affairs (MOFA) for selectively targeting its requests for assistance "based on needs." Rather than appealing for blanket international assistance, Japan's government looked to OCHA and other international actors for complementary efforts and "carefully selected the assistance it needed to support national response efforts."[65] Bearing the brunt of the responsibility for repairing infrastructure and providing disaster relief within Japan was the Ministry of Land, Infrastructure, Transport, and Tourism (MLIT). Responsible for the clearing of roads, ports, airports, railways, and rivers in addition to securing emergency housing for those affected by the disaster, MLIT's eminently successful execution of infrastructure recovery was but one example of Japan's bureaucratic efficiency. MLIT established its emergency headquarters approximately 30 minutes after the disaster and was well on its way to accomplishing all of the goals of its Operation Toothcomb, a plan that called for the clearance of 97 percent of Japan's national roads and expressways leading to the impacted areas.[66] MLIT's planners diverted much if not all of the rail traffic from the Tohoku JR line to lines along the Japan Sea and facilitated deliveries of

---

[65] "OCHA 2011 Annual Report," 3.

[66] Ministry of Land, Infrastructure, Transport and Tourism presentation titled "MLIT's Emergency Response to the Great East Japan Earthquake," slide 13, accessed October 3, 2012, http://www.mlit.go.jp/river/basic_info/english/conference.html.

petroleum to affected areas in order to ease severe fuel shortages.[67] More than 500 MLIT personnel on liaison and technical assistance teams were dispatched to affected areas in order to conduct surveys, restore telecommunications capabilities, and assist in averaging a 3-day response time to all requests for humanitarian relief supplies to include clothing washers, lavatories, and temporary housing.[68] It would be a fair assessment to claim that the Ministry of Land, Infrastructure, Transport and Tourism is a competent governmental agency that reacted appropriately and with great haste in assisting the victims of 2011's earthquake and tsunami in Japan.

Moving away from government ministries, the Japanese Red Cross Society (JRCS) was exceedingly capable in its response to the March 11 disasters. Responsible for distributing over 231 billion Yen in Japanese donations amongst affected citizens, the JRCS rapidly undertook its various tasks of establishing field clinics, directly treating ill or injured persons, as well as liaise with MLIT officials in procuring and equipping replacement shelters. Only 30 days after the disaster, 452 medical teams had been deployed from the JRCS network of 93 hospitals, 26 of which were operating in the three most heavily damaged prefectures of Miyagi, Fukushima and Iwate. By April 12th 34,430 patients had been treated by the JRCS.[69] Psychological and trauma support teams were working alongside relief teams while the organization implemented a plan to equip up to 70,000 replacement shelters with home appliances, regenerators, washing machine, rice cooker, microwave, and a television.[70] By May 6th, approximately 55,739 patients had been treated by JRCS medical teams and 132,510 blankets, 183,000 pieces of clothing, and 30,132 emergency relief kits had been distributed by the Japanese relief agency to its own citizens.[71] Suffice to say, the response by Japanese relief agencies to

---

[67] Ibid., 17.

[68] Ibid., 22.

[69] "Japan: Earthquake and Tsunami Operations Update No. 1," Japanese Red Cross Society, April 13 2011, accessed June 2, 2012. http://reliefweb.int/report/japan/earthquake-and-tsunami-operations-update-n°-1.

[70] Ibid.

[71] "Japan: Earthquake and Tsunami Operations Update No. 2," Japanese Red Cross Society, May 6, 2011, accessed June 2, 2012. http://reliefweb.int/report/japan/earthquake-and-tsunami-operations-update-n°-2.

the 2011 disaster was timely, appropriate, and effective in its role as the primary assisting agent to affected Japanese citizens, so much so that the International Medical Corps 1 Year Report on Japan complemented the nation on its "significant disaster response capability."[72]

2. Host Nation Military Capabilities

The Japanese Self Defense Force (JSDF) owes much of its humanitarian relief capabilities to its founding legacy, a heritage that former Prime Minister Shigeru Yoshida predicted in 1957 would bring the JSDF "appreciation and praise" for its "disaster relief missions."[73] Familiar with its role of a capable force within the framework of peacekeeping or disaster relief operations, the JSDF met the challenges of the 2011 earthquake and tsunami with ample capability, resources, and efficacy. Broaching new operational territory in some respects while reaffirming proficiencies in other areas, the actions undertaken by all of the components of the JSDF did much to assuage domestic and international observers of skepticism of its abilities to respond effectively in a crisis.

The mobilization of the JSDF in the wake of the March 11th disaster was significant on two fronts; first, over 100,000 personnel were mobilized in what would be the largest response within its history, and second, it marked the first time a task force had been established amongst the maritime, air, and ground components of the Japanese Self Defense Force.[74] JSDF reservists were activated for the first time in recent history and by March 18th, over 545 aircraft and 54 ships were directly participating within the disaster response. Defense Force personnel continue the MILT and JRCS missions of providing emergency relief, shelter, and equipment on an emergency basis.[75] Additional data detailing JSDF effectiveness within the disaster can be found in Table 2.

---

[72] "Japan 1 Year Report," *International Medical Corps*, 1.

[73] Alex Martin, "Military Flexes Relief Might," *Japan Times*, April 15, 2011.

[74] "Defense of Japan 2012," Japan's Ministry of Defense White Paper, 2012, 213, accessed September 2, 2012, http://www.mod.go.jp/e/publ/w_paper/2012.html.

[75] Ibid., 211.

	Activity	Total
Rescue, etc	Lifesaving	19,286 people
	Recovery of deceased	9,505 bodies
	Transportation of deceased	1,004 bodies
Transportation	Transportation of goods	13,906 t
	Transportation of medical teams, etc.	20,240 people
	Transportation of patients	175 patients
Livelihood assistance	Water supply assistance	32,985t (maximum of approx. 200 locations)
	Food assistance	5,005,484 servings (maximum of approx. 100 locations)
	Fuel assistance	1,606 KL
	Bathing assistance	1,092,585 people (maximum of 35 locations)
	Sanitation assistance	22,653 people

Table 1. Self-Defense Force Statistics (From Japan's Ministry of Defense White Paper, 2012).

In the wake of the disaster, the JSDF received a considerable amount of public commendation and appreciation for its actions within a humanitarian relief role. Any number of newspapers editorials called for the defense forces to "be involved continually in relief activities" for the foreseeable future and the fact that activated reservists were visible in the community directly assisting their hometown and neighbors was a dynamic not lost on the Japanese public.[76] It would therefore be a fair assessment to make that the Japanese Self Defense Force was appropriately postured and resourced to responds to a domestic humanitarian scenario.

E.   CONCLUSION

This chapter provided a glimpse of U.S. disaster relief efforts within the context of the 2011 earthquake and tsunami in Japan. Understood now to be one of the world's most severe and costly earthquakes, the magnitude 9.0 event directly affected one of the

---

[76] "SDF Should Enhance Disaster Relief Role," *The Daily Yomiuri*, March 21, 2011.

United States' staunchest allies and security partners, a partner within which the U.S. forward deploys nearly 40,000 military personnel. While the large presence of U.S. service members prior to the March 11 event may have led to what was a considerable response, the requests for military assistance as observed through USAID's OFDA and the Joint Requirements Review Board was in fact limited to only 48. Finally, the chapter ended by touching on the two predictive variables that I feel to be most beneficial for foreign militaries rendering humanitarian assistance in a foreign country. The actions taken by Japan's Ministry of Land, Infrastructure, Transport and Tourism and the Japanese Red Cross Society were robust and also notably within the expected norms for an OECD developed nation such as Japan. Furthermore, the Japanese Self Defense Force's superlative efforts in assisting its citizens within this humanitarian scenario reaffirmed its legacy as a civil-relief agency and should serve to inform the international community on its future capabilities.

IV.   NORTHERN INDONESIA EARTHQUAKE AND TSUNAMI (2004)

A.   INTRODUCTION

On December 26, 2004, a magnitude 9.0 earthquake struck beneath the seabed of the Indian Ocean approximately 120 miles off the coast of Banda Aceh, Sumatra, Indonesia. The massive quake sent a number of tsunami waves toward 12 countries across the Indian Ocean, the largest of which hit the western coast of Sumatra across 300 miles of beaches within the province of Aceh.[77] Within this chapter I discuss the scope and severity of this natural disaster in the context of its devastating effect upon the Aceh province of Indonesia, as well as assess whether the U.S. maritime response was appropriately scaled to the disaster and in recognition of the previously referenced predictive variables. Just one of nearly 35 nations committing military assets to address the wide spectrum of needs, the United States' maritime military assets, its respective command structures, and its coordination with USAID OFDA officials were extremely important to understanding the efficacy and appropriateness of the effort. Following this I will discuss the actions and relative competence of Indonesia's civil relief institutions as well as the actions of the Indonesian Armed Forces (Tentera Nasional Indonesia, TNI), as each of these constitute a predictive variable that I feel are the two most important assessment factors for U.S. military planners to understand as they attempt to render balanced and effective aid within foreign humanitarian operations.

---

[77] "The Effectiveness of Foreign Military Assets," 87.

B.   SCOPE OF THE DISASTER

The depths of the disaster within the Indonesian province of Aceh were not immediately realized following the tsunami's strike ashore due in part to the affected area's remote location, lack of established infrastructure, as well as the general state of insecurity due to an ongoing counter-insurgency operation between the TNI and members of the Free Aceh Movement. Yet as media attention effectively illuminated the full brunt of the impact of the earthquake and tsunami on Indonesia, the international community would soon realize that aid would be required that fell far beyond Indonesia's capability. The massive earthquake itself released an equivalent amount of energy as found between 0.25 and 0.8 gigatons of TNT. The following tsunami released enough energy to equal nearly 23,000 Hiroshima level atom bombs. [78] Solely within the confines of Indonesia, the disaster led to a material loss of close to $445 million U.S. dollars with nearly 60 percent of this figure coming from property damage. Government data indicated in 2005 that 124,946 Indonesians lost their lives with 94,994 still missing. Owing much to the poor pre-existing construction and itinerant families, at least 400,376 individuals in Aceh were displaced by the disaster and the distribution of the internally displaced population can be found below within Figure 4. [79]

---

[78] Bruce A. Elleman, *Waves of Hope: The U.S. Navy's Response to the Tsunami in Northern Indonesia*, (Newport, Rhode Island: Naval War College Press, 2007), 1.

[79] "After the Tsunami: Human Rights of Vulnerable Populations," Human Rights Center, University of California Berkley, October 2005, 26.

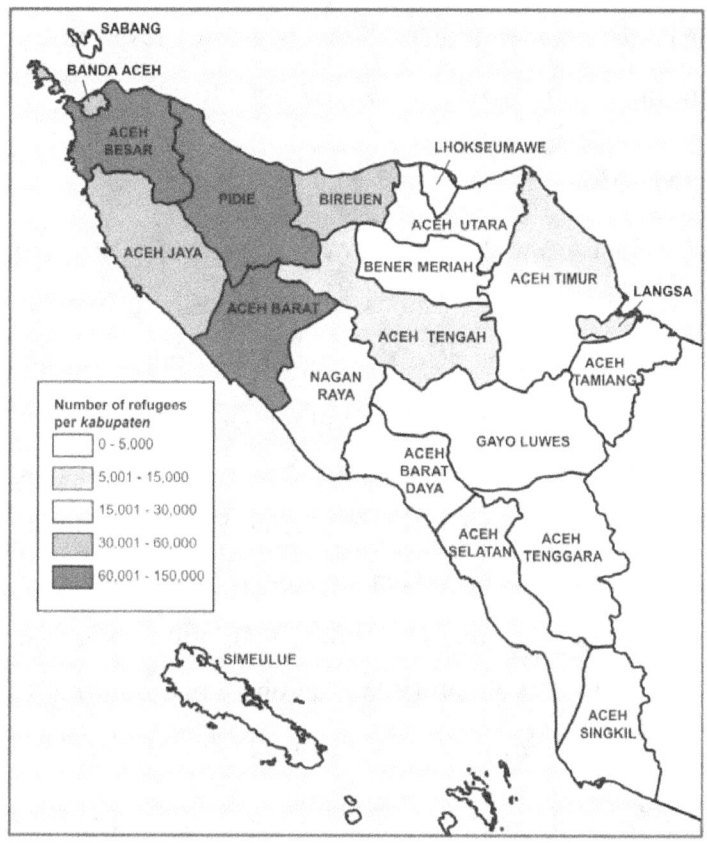

Figure 4.   Map of IDP Distribution (From Human Rights Center, 2005).

Communications networks and even the local control stations for satellite systems were drastically impacted within Aceh province. Because most people in the province lived close to the coast, access to the western coast of the province proved nearly impossible due to the losses of existing roads, bridges, airstrips, and even harbors. The sole major airport in the region, located in the capital, Banda Aceh, was massively impacted and only regained partial functionality as disaster relief efforts progressed. As a result, foreign militaries and aid agencies were forced to utilize the airport in Medan, nearly 300 miles away.[80] The requirements for air mobility would become increasingly important in the days following the disaster. Lacking serviceable airports, overland logistics routes, and an organic communications network, the ability to muster helicopters to assess, survey, and delivery relief supplies would become the most important asset due

---

[80] "The Effectiveness of Foreign Military Assets," 87.

to the nature of the operational space following this disaster. Therefore, the massive scope and uniquely devastating affect of the tsunami presented numerous logistical concerns that maritime capability was "uniquely suited to address."[81]

C.   U.S. RESPONSE

The unique affect of the damage as well as a few concerns from the host nation facilitated a unique U.S. maritime response to the disaster in Indonesia. These actions were just a small part of a larger, PACOM-initiated effort to facilitate relief by using military capabilities across the whole of Southeast Asia. Responding promptly to what was then a varied reporting of severity amongst the international media, Admiral Thomas Fargo as the commander of U.S. Pacific Command established Joint Task Force (JTF) 536 under the command of Lieutenant General Robert R. Blackman, Jr., who at that time commanded the 3rd Marine Expeditionary Force (MEF) on Okinawa, Japan.[82] Due in part to consideration toward the multilateral actions that would be necessary given the immense size of this disaster, PACOM planners shifted the JTF nomenclature to Combined Support Force (CSF) 536 on January 3 which complemented the stated PACOM mission of providing "assistance to the governments of Indonesia, Sri Lanka, Thailand and other affected nations to mitigate the effects of the recent earthquake and tsunami in the Indian Ocean."[83] In addition to the Combined Support Staff in Utapao, PACOM's own Multinational Planning Augmentation Team (MPAT) was established within the same compound in order to host military liaison officers from a variety of other nations that were participating in the disaster relief effort. It was within this MPAT team that requests for assistance that could not be sourced to U.S. assets was met by assisting foreign nations.[84] First established in 2000, PACOM's MPAT initiative has

---

[81] Jessica Piombo and Michael Malley, "Beyond Protecting the Land and the Sea: The Role of the U.S. Navy in Reconstruction," in *Naval Peacekeeping and Humanitarian Operations: Stability from the Sea*, ed. James J. Wirtz and Jeffrey A. Larsen. (New York: Routledge, 2009), 73.

[82] Elleman, *Waves of Hope*, 8.

[83] Ibid, 29.

[84] Tom Frey, "Assignment as the USAID-OFDA DART Leader to Operation Unified Assistance Joint Task Force/Combined Support Force – 536 for Earthquake/Tsunami Relief Efforts Utapao, Thailand 29 December, 2004 – 2 February 2005," Lessons Learned by DART Leader. www.wildfirelessons.net, accessed December 11, 2012.

continually sought to promote better understandings of disaster management and emergency response systems within a multilateral setting and was instrumental in harnessing the vast array of partner capabilities within the larger scope of the 2004 Indian Ocean earthquake and tsunami.

Because the United States participates in the annual COBRA GOLD exercises in Thailand, CSF 536 personnel found it quite appropriate to establish the same logistical headquarters in Utapao, Thailand, at the Royal Thai Navy Base known as "Red Horse." As this central spoke was being quickly established in early January, a number of disaster relief assessment teams (DRAT) established their respective command structure in Thailand, Sri Lanka, and Indonesia. The official CSF representative was headquartered in Medan, Indonesia, just outside of Aceh province, under the command of U.S. Marine Corps Brigadier General Christian B. Cowdrey from the 3rd Marine Division in Okinawa, Japan. Yet as seen through much of the damage and geography, Medan was not convenient for military planners to render assistance to affected areas. For this reason and also possibly recognizing his status as senior to Brigadier General Cowdrey, Rear Admiral Douglas Crowder aboard the *USS ABRAHAM LINCOLN* and the head of his Carrier Strike Group was "for all practical purposes in charge of the operation in Indonesia."[85] The CSF 536 task organization can additionally be seen below within Figure 5.

---

[85] Ibid, 32.

CSF-536 Task Organization

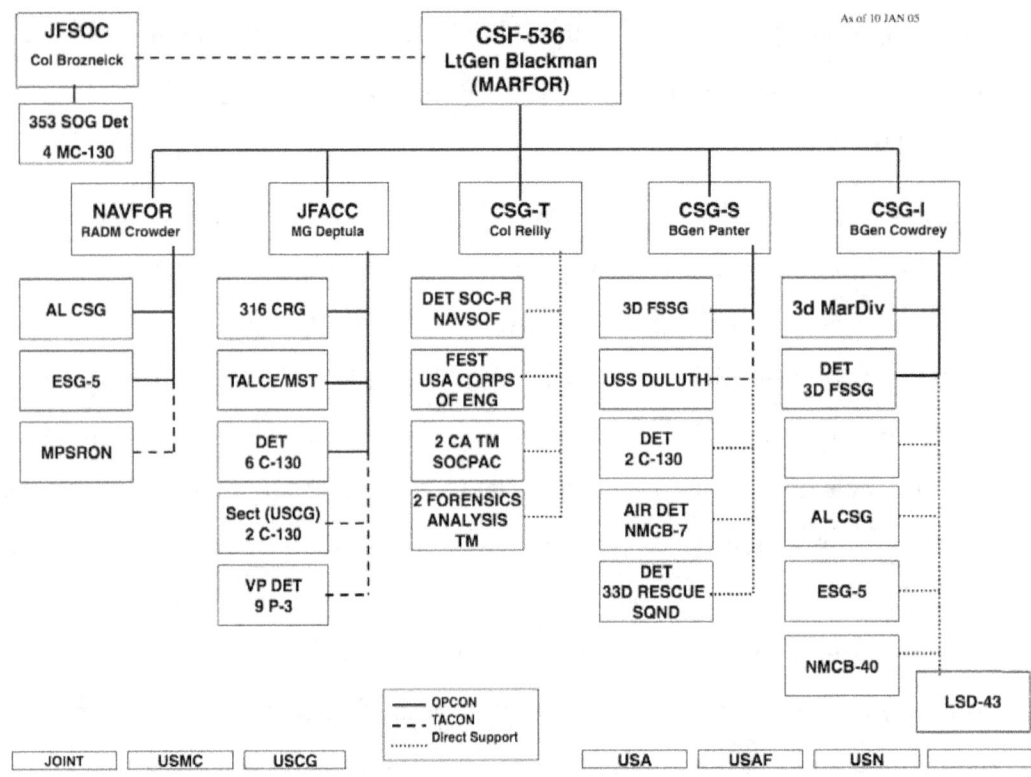

Figure 5.   CSF-536 Task Organization (From Office of History,
Pacific Air Forces, 2005).

As the commander of Carrier Strike Group 9, which on the eve of the disaster in Indonesia was berthed in Hong Kong, Rear Admiral Crowder was best positioned to provide the most immediate relief to the area. President Bush detailed the initial U.S. response within his address to the press on December 29 when he said that "we're dispatching a Marine expeditionary unit, the aircraft carrier *ABRAHAM LINCOLN*, and the maritime pre-position squadron from Guam to the area to help with relief efforts."[86] The value of maritime assets and their operational "sea-basing" plan was seen as ever more important and effective when understanding that the prompt presence of the *ABRAHAM LINCOLN*, as well as the *USS BONHOMME RICHARD*, allowed for over twenty-five ships, forty-five fixed wing aircraft, and fifty-eight helicopters were on-scene

[86] Ibid, 22.

44

delivering more than 610,000 pounds of food and water by January 5, a mere two days after PACOM had finally decided on the operation's nomenclature.[87]

As the airport in Banda Aceh remained inoperable, the minimum logistical footprint provided by maritime assets became even more crucial. Combined with ongoing force protection concerns in Aceh province due to the ongoing insurgency, the promise of U.S. troops not setting up base camps ashore was well suited for host nation concerns of cultural and religious uncertainty due to the perceived mission of Christians within the American military soldiers to convert an Islamic populace.[88] All told, the U.S. Navy's ability to remain offshore "decreased the American footprint, reduced friction, and so greatly facilitated the missions objectives."[89]

As helicopter crews began their first relief mission on January 2, maritime planners sought to paint this mission as a combined effort with a significant Indonesian presence. These crews had the foresight to include a member of the TNI within their flight crews and aboard their helicopters so as to acknowledge that the Indonesian representative was clearly "in charge."[90] This embarked TNI member would serve to organize survivors once on the ground, unload supplies, and generally oversee distribution. This conscious effort toward bilateralism was continued ashore by positioning "one Indonesian soldier, then one American" anytime relief supplies were passed amongst the populace.[91]

All told, approximately 12,000 U.S. service members and over 17 ships participated in the maritime response to the Indonesian earthquake and tsunami.[92] A more complete listing of the responding maritime assets can be found below:

- ABRAHAM LINCOLN Carrier Strike Group, 5 Escorts (CRUDES)
- Carrier Air Wing 2

---

[87] Ibid, 10.

[88] Ibid, 37.

[89] Ibid, 38.

[90] Ibid, 58.

[91] Ibid, 58.

[92] Ibid, 23.

- BONHOMME RICHARD Expeditionary Strike Group, 6 Escorts
- 17 Logistical Support Ships
- 8 Squadrons providing 58 helicopters[93]

It was these same assets that flew "1,800 sorties, delivered 2,700 tons of food, water and medicine and evacuated 3,000 people" from affected areas within Aceh province.[94] As U.S. naval forces in the *Abraham Lincoln* CSG operated within Indonesian waters for roughly four weeks until they departed the area on February 3, 2012, the effectiveness of their presence was increasingly realized through their unique capabilities that suited the nature of the Indonesian disaster. The U.S. Navy was restricted in its main focus due to the short duration of the operation by emphasizing life-sustaining water, food, and medicine instead of emphasizing basic infrastructure recovery. Due consideration was paid to the type of destruction present within Aceh province and the lack of crucial transportation and communication infrastructure, combined with the lack of the host nation's own boats and docking equipment, led rescuers and relief agencies to create "their own logistical flow, access, communications, and medical services, and only sea-based naval forces can do so."[95] As water was one of the most vital relief supplies required for the refugee population immediately following the disaster, airdrops were not a practical delivery method for rendering assistance. As we understand the nature and scope of the disaster, we can see that despite the relatively short duration of the U.S. response, the actions of maritime forces were suited to the needs and demands of the operational space of the humanitarian scenario as well as the varied requests for assistance from the Indonesian government. Understanding this, I would assert that the U.S. maritime response to the Aceh disaster in 2004 was conclusively effective, not excessive in nature, and well suited to the needs of the Indonesian government. I will continue this evaluation of efficacy within the concluding chapter as I draw parallels to the 2011 Japan case study.

---

[93] Ibid, 33.

[94] Ibid, 92.

[95] Ibid, 112.

1. Coordination with USAID

Just as the maritime components of the U.S. military were preparing to respond to the Indonesian disaster, so too were civilians from USAID's Office of Foreign Disaster Assistance (OFDA). Nearly 150 civilians were mobilized to CSF headquarters in Utapao and across the Pacific in order to facilitate the "rapid delivery of live-and-death aid to Aceh province."[96] Taken from an OFDA DART Utapao memo, the role of the USAID military liaison cells within the Indonesian operation was to validate and prioritize "the requests for assistance to ensure limited and scarce USG resources are used in the most effective and efficient manner."[97] This request for assistance (RFA) process pre-dates the JRRB structure seen in Operation Tomadachi yet served much the same purpose. The success of the RFA process lead to later calls for the formalization and acceptance of what was seen in Japan in 2011. The Utapao memo continues by stipulating that any RFAs should be submitted to the respective CSF representative through an OFDA/DART Military Liaison Officer who was located, in this instance, in both Medan and Banda Aceh.[98] These requests were to be received with an underlying understanding that "military and civil defense assets should be seen as a tool complementing existing relief mechanisms," much in accordance with the Oslo Guidelines.

In order to meet this guidance, a maritime planner from the ABRAHAM LINCOLN attended a meeting ashore each evening at 7 o'clock during which Military Liaison Officers and relief organizations determined what supplies were needed and where they needed to go the next day. Following this, the carrier's flight schedule was designed to reflect the previous day's inputs and to ensure that the priorities of assisting maritime military assets were in line with those of relief agencies ashore.[99]

This level of integration between U.S. naval assets and USAID representatives was exemplary, so much so that a USAID Military Liaison Unit after action report held it

---

[96] Ibid, 39.

[97] "Request for Military Assistance (RFA) Procedure," DRAFT: USAID/OFDA/DART Utapao. Policy memo received September 4, 2012 from OFDA representative Tom Fray.

[98] Ibid.

[99] Elleman, *Waves of Hope*, 52.

to be "one of the best examples of an effective collaboration between OFDA and the military."[100] This report did continue in its affirmation of the collaboration by calling for formalization of the RFA process "within DoD and other USG agencies in order to more rapidly apply the process to future contingencies."[101] This impetus for a structured and formalized framework would later become the JRRB/MITAM initiatives as seen within Operation Tomodachi.

D. PREDICTIVE VARIABLES

As discussed previously in Chapter II, I hold two predictive variables as most important for military planners as they attempt to understand the operational space prior to providing humanitarian relief in a foreign nation. It is the dynamic nature of a humanitarian affairs operation and the fundamentally different ways in which the operation evolves that makes these scenarios different from typical military operations, all of which emphasizes the need for military planners to properly address and understand the operational space prior to the commencement of relief operations. Of these fundamentally different dynamics, I hold that a nations civil relief capabilities and organic military capabilities present the biggest game changing dynamics for assisting foreign militaries. Pre-existing strengths or weakness within either host nation institution serve to drastically shape the form that such foreign aid will take and in this instance I will discuss how Indonesia's civil relief institutions and military shaped the respective U.S. maritime response.

The responses from Indonesia's civil relief organizations and military to the disaster scenario were by many accounts mixed and it is important to fully understand the security dynamic in Aceh province prior to the events of December 26. With the ongoing conflict between the TNI and Free Aceh Movement, there had been a significant number of previously reported human rights violations on both sides. While martial law had been lifted the previous May, the province remained within an official state of civil

---

100 "Disaster Response MLU After-Action Report," Indian Ocean Earthquake/Tsunami Reponse, 1. Report received September 4, 2012 from OFDA representative Tom Fray.

101 Ibid, 2.

emergency. TNI commanders had previously mandated that all visiting non-governmental organizations be provided military escorts lest more security incidents occur.[102] These outlying areas were places where "traditionally those in uniform were not/are not viewed as a benign presence."[103] While tensions between the Indonesian population and members of the TNI did run quite high due to the tense security situation, it is important to note that hostilities were largely halted following the disaster due to the vast devastation sustained by both sides of the conflict. Both TNI and GAM forces sustained losses to personnel and logistics due to the tsunami and the immediate focus after 26 December was to provide relief, regardless the affiliation. These underlying tensions, however, do play a role in some of the methods relief agencies and the TNI accounted for and distributed relief supplies within the immediate response phase of the disaster scenario. It was within this dynamic security environment that U.S. military planners were forced to operate during this wide-ranging humanitarian disaster.

1. Civil Relief Institutions

Perhaps the overriding themes derived from the actions of Indonesia's civil relief institutions during the humanitarian response could be described as confusion and a general lack of resources. Indonesia's National Coordinating Body for Disaster Management (Badan Koordinasi Nasional Penanggulangan Bencana dan Penanganan Pengungsi, BAKORNAS PBP) was responsible for coordinating the state's actions during disaster relief.[104] The confusion began early in the relief process as the competing command structures within Aceh, the tattered existing regional government, the civil emergency military commander, and the Satkorlak (the provincial representative of BAKORNAS), all felt as though they should take the lead in the effort while all seemingly lacked the capability to do so.[105]

---

[102] "The Effectiveness of Foreign Military Assets," 88.

[103] Clare Harkin, "The 2004 Tsunami: Civil Military Aspects of the International Response," Tsunami Evaluation Coalition, Coordination of International Humanitarian Assistance in Tsunami-Affected Countries, 2004, 3.

[104] "The Effectiveness of Foreign Military Assets," 89.

[105] "After the Tsunami," 32.

49

Regardless of its legal authority, BAKORNAS officials were clearly overwhelmed and unprepared for the massive scale of the disaster. Despite its formal structure on both national and provincial levels, the organization lacked any real assets or implementation authority. Levels of outreach across the provincial level were varied and its presence was far from institutionalized.

2.   Host Nation Military Capabilities

Just as I briefly addressed the Japanese Self-Defense Force's legacy of providing direct assistance to its people, I would like to touch on the larger preoccupation with domestic security within Indonesian society. Understanding the unique security conflict within Aceh province prior to the disaster in late 2004, I am utilizing Indonesia's passage of Law No. 34 in 2004 in order to garner an idea of their perceived role in serving the Indonesian people before remarking on their actions subsequent to the tsunami.

The TNI's role within the over-arching state security apparatus in Indonesia is a large one and its reach into domestic matters is directly representative the Indonesian government's obsession with non-traditional security threats from within the country while wholly accepting that "external physical threats to sovereignty are unlikely."[106] The Ministry of Defense 2003 White Paper goes far in addressing domestic security issues and complements the pre-existing territorial system employed by the central government to administer its vast archipelagic claims within South East Asia. The text continues to talk in great depth of countering the GAM and similar movements with the full support and aid of Indonesia's populace but spends very little time addressing its role within a civil humanitarian disaster. The idea of such a robust humanitarian relief role was less than fully developed as also evidenced in its relative lack of organization or initiative to serve the Indonesian people following the disaster on 26 December. Quite notable however, was the decline in antagonistic behavior between TNI and the Free

---

[106] "Defending the Country Entering the 21st Century," Indonesia White Paper, March 2003, VII.

Aceh movement following the disaster, a status that was likely due to recent peace negotiations as well as the emphasis placed on rendering humanitarian aid to all effected persons.[107]

Having addressed the TNI's role within the country's territorial system, I will now look at the TNI's stated role within disaster relief scenarios. Law No. 34 stipulated specifically that the TNI should "assist in coping with natural disaster relief, evacuation, and humanitarian assistance."[108] It was this recently adopted law that allowed for the TNI to take a more active role in Military Operations Other Than War (MOOTW) and would be crucial as a foundation for the organizations actions following the events of December 26.

Reports concerning the efficacy of TNI members within the disaster relief effort bear mixed results. With over 45,000 security personnel deployed to the province prior to the event due to ongoing security operations, one could expect a likely rapid and robust response.[109] Despite suffering a large number of casualties within its own ranks, the TNI was reportedly "the only surviving governmental structure" and they took the lead on clearing debris, evacuating victims, opening roads, and building the aforementioned barracks.[110] It was the TNI's own commander, General Endriartono Sutarto, who requested direct assistance within the humanitarian disaster from his counterparts in Australia, Malaysia, New Zealand, Singapore, and the United States.[111] A number of reports have commended Indonesia's for its openness and flexibility in receiving foreign military assistance within its sovereign territory, a significant act that some say led to saving many of the refugees.

While the TNI's actions within the immediate response phase of the disaster relief operation were commendable in some respects, there were a considerable number of

---

[107] Piombo and Malley, "Beyond," 74.

[108] "The Role of TNI in Disaster Management," Presentation by B.G. Syaifun Anwar for the United Nations Office for the Coordination of Humanitarian Affairs, Jakarta, May 23, 2011.

[109] Piombo and Malley, "Beyond," 74.

[110] "After the Tsunami," 32.

[111] "The Effectiveness of Foreign Military Assets," 91.

reports of abuse as well. Aceh regional executive Bambang Antariksa criticized the opening stages of the rescue effort when he remarked on the lack of any rescue operation within the opening days for "survivors who were buried under the debris."[112] Additionally, evacuation priority from the affected area within some parts of Aceh province was seen to favor family members of the security forces. The looting of gold jewelry from deceased Acehnese women by local military commanders led one survivor from Lamno District to comment "perhaps that's why the military guarding us were very interested when we said the corpse was female."[113]

Clearly the military's presence in Aceh during the relief efforts was viewed by affected Indonesians as less than magnanimous on some occasions and I think it would be reasonable to say that the TNI was unprepared and overwhelmed by the scale of the disaster following the 26 December earthquake and tsunami. Despite its understood and widely accepted role in providing domestic disaster relief within situations such as the 2004 tsunami, the TNI was hindered by its lack of mobility and aerial lift that would have been well suited to this disaster scenario, capabilities that U.S. maritime forces were uniquely positioned to provide. The Indonesian territorial system referenced earlier in the chapter left the TNI as a military body that was incapable of fluid movement and dynamic response as necessary within this situation. The TNI did, however, function commendably well in hosting foreign military capability within Indonesian borders and worked to facilitate access to the effected population.

E.   CONCLUSION

This chapter provided a glimpse of U.S. disaster relief efforts in the context of the 2004 earthquake and tsunami off of Aceh province, Indonesia. Impacting a region of Indonesia that was already plagued by internal conflict and a poor civic infrastructure, the 9.0 magnitude earthquake and sprawling tsunami-impact area necessitated the presence of foreign military relief efforts from 35 countries. Nearly 13,000 U.S. military members assisted from the sea by utilizing USAID OFDA Military Liaison Officers to effectively

---

[112] "After the Tsunami," 32.

[113] Ibid, 33.

assess and validate host nation needs through a robust RFA process. In conclusion, this chapter discussed the two predictive variables that I feel most accurately reflect the likelihood for genuine need of foreign military assistance, the efficacy of host nation civil relief institutions and its own military capabilities. Failings in the disaster relief responses within each of these organizations led to a robust U.S. effort that was in turn appropriate and effective. The rampant confusion and reported instances of abuse from the efforts of Indonesia's own relief bureaucracy and military disaster relief efforts portend the respective organizations lack of ability to effectively render aid, thus creating operational space for foreign militaries to respond.

THIS PAGE INTENTIONALLY LEFT BLANK

V. CONCLUDING REMARKS

A. INTRODUCTION

Any operation to provide foreign military assistance to a disaster relief scenario remains far from an exact science. Yet while we understand that while each likely scenario in the future will be unique to the host nation and disaster, I hold that there are a number of common factors that can be derived from examining similar operations within which U.S. maritime assets have rendered disaster aid. The United States provided maritime assets to assist within the 2004 Aceh earthquake and tsunami as well as the 2011 Great Japan earthquake and tsunami. These cases are important for a number of reasons and I intend to use this chapter to draw sharp parallels that speak to instances of excess maritime capacity as well as the ways in which I assess such instances. Furthermore, these assessments of excess maritime capacity in turn reflect the importance of understanding and appreciating the previously mentioned predictive variables, two factors that I will discuss respective to each case study. I will then touch on a number of reason U.S. maritime planners may have proffered such excess capacity in these situations, and review any pertinent recommendations for U.S. policy change, if any. Finally, I will conclude this chapter with a research overview that will reexamine this research's significance, likely shortfalls, and areas for further study.

B. ANALYSIS AND KEY FINDINGS

The disasters of 2004 and 2011 were similar in their magnitude as well as their respective scale of U.S. maritime assistance. Understanding that geographic placement, the presence of early warning systems, and urban planning and development largely accounted for the discrepancy between the two events in terms of deceased and displaced persons, the two events were similarly expensive in terms of capital expended during recovery and reconstruction. Within each, the inherent mobility of maritime assets was invaluable to the opening stages of search and recovery, a period of time early in a disaster relief scenario termed earlier within this paper as a time for "immediate relief." While a number of sources have agreed that military assistance early within this recovery process is invaluable and apropos for foreign militaries to undertake, there is a definite recognition of the tendency for military operations to move beyond the bounds of their mission as bounded by U.S. joint publications, internationally accepted norms and guidance, and operationally specific tasking orders, and fill any perceived operational space.

Lieutenant Colonel James Daniel has written an excellent article for Military Review in regards to tsunami transitions, in this instance the event in 2004, which led me to my measure of effectiveness and assessment of excess capacity. LTC Daniels recounts the choices facing the commander of Combined Support Force 536 in 2005 as it became time to transition forces away from the relief mission. Outside of established measures of effectiveness and achievement of International Red Cross Sphere Standards of Habitation Environments, the commander on the ground in Utapao opted instead to pinpoint a minimum number of requests for assistance "since a declining number would seem to indicate less need for military assistance."[114]   This intuitive direct relationship, a declining value of RFAs as a directly representative of assessed need, seemed to be the most universal and easily reproduced evaluation of the necessity of a continued military presence within a disaster relief scenario. This fundamental grasp of gauging need and requirements seems ever more pertinent when one understands that the RFA process as facilitated by USAID OFDA consciously reflects the norms and principles held through the Oslo Guidelines, the same principles that restrict military actions those endeavors that are complimentary to the host nation and undertaken as a 'last resort'.

Utilizing this same measure of effectiveness, I find it impossible to reconcile the presence of 15,000 U.S. military service members within the maritime component in Japan for the events of 2011, approximately 2,000 more than were present in 2004 in Aceh, with the 48 validated MITAMs or validated requests for DoD assistance as anything other than excessive. In addition to this discrepancy, I have noted a number of instance where I believe the services rendered or at least attempted by U.S. maritime assets during the 2011 recovery efforts was not complementary nor desired. The Port

---

[114] James Daniel, "Operation Unified Assistance: Tsunami Transitions," *Military Review*, January-February 2006, 53.

Clearance Group encountered more than one local government that chose not to utilize its services due to an existing organic capability. The RFA and MITAM process is invaluable in another sense because provides the benefit of cataloging all military aid that was rendered beneath the auspices of humanitarian assistance. With this perspective, one can easily see how a community relations project initiative approximately 20 days after the 11 March disaster could be described as excessive and not seen beneath a humanitarian mandate.

With the understanding that U.S. maritime assistance within the 2011 disaster relief was on occasion excessive and scaled beyond the required needs of the host nation, I will continue to explain the value of the two predictive variables as well as other reasons why this excessive response may have occurred.

1.   Value of Predictive Variables

I believe one reason U.S. maritime planners may have responded to the 2011 Japan disaster with excess capacity lies within a failure to properly assess the unique operational environment of a humanitarian mission, an environment that is drastically different from the other types of missions the U.S. military typically encounters. United States Joint Publication 3–29 which governs the use of Foreign Humanitarian Assistance reflects my concerns as well and calls for a "different mindset and different techniques" when assessing the operational space prior to executing any sort of mission.[115]

My previously mentioned predictive variables, the proficiency of host nation civil relief institutions as well as military capabilities, similarly reflect Joint Publication 3–29 first two recommended assessment factors for humanitarian operations. Understanding the status and intent of military or paramilitary forces within an effected nation as well as determining the relevant governmental actors within an operational area are two tasks that can greatly shape the expected efforts of any mission. The proficiency exhibited by Japan's MLIT and Self-Defense Forces was could have been expected considering Japan's high degree of infrastructure development and history of engagement with the U.S. military. As proficient as the Japanese Red Cross Society was within the 2011

---

[115] "Foreign Humanitarian Assistance," III-7.

disaster, I believe U.S. military planners should have been able to adopt a more complimentary role that would have been in accordance with accepted Oslo Guidelines. Similarly, as U.S. planners lacked an established record of engagement with Indonesia's TNI prior to 2004, it should have been clearly apparent that the host nation would likely request the United States to adopt a more robust role in the effort, which I believe we did accomplish well and to the best of our abilities through an appropriate and efficient utilization of military assets.

2.   U.S. Maritime Forces as the Primary Agent for Relief

One factor that I believe may have played a role within leading maritime forces to respond with excess capacity is their primacy within the planning and execution of a disaster relief operation. I would claim that in instances where U.S. maritime planners are obligated in the basic, bilateral organization of rendering aid, planners take away a more accurate assessment of need and provide thusly. The 2004 relief operation found the U.S. Navy as the de facto lead for CSF-Indonesia despite a USMC Brigadier General in Medan. This owed much to the geography and remote dislocation of much of the effected area as well as the fact that U.S. Navy rotary winged assets were effectively the only game in town when it came to direct delivery of aid. This primacy within the planning process allowed maritime planners to attend daily meeting with OFDA Military Liaison Officers ashore before crafting the next day's flight plan, thereby correlating USAID's humanitarian goals with U.S. Navy efforts as evidenced by the massively successful RFA process.

Within Operation Tomodachi, U.S. maritime planners were largely left to their own devices aboard USS RONALD REAGAN and USS ESSEX, at least when it came to planning their own relief missions into the effected areas of Japan's coastal areas. The ongoing validation process within OFDA's Joint Requirements Review Board was conducted from Yokota Air Base each evening and then disseminated to service component representative who lacked even a basic secure network to communicate with operational forces afloat. Representatives within the Bilateral Joint Operations Center in Yokota often times has no visibility on aid flight missions until the day's flight hours and statistics were posted within each evening's operational briefing. I feel as though this lack of constant oversight led to a mindset where U.S. naval units sought to maximize humanitarian efforts in assistance to Japan by utilizing all possible forces despite the obvious need for a demand signal from Japanese Joint Staff planners. This perceived gap between the relief agency assessment perspective and the operationally driven providers could potentially prove disasters in future situations when encountering perhaps a more dynamic security environment than seen in Japan in 2011.

3.   U.S. Navy and Japanese Maritime Self-Defense Force Familiarity

I believe the U.S. Navy's preexisting relationship and operational familiarity with the Japanese Maritime Self Defense force lent itself toward a dynamic maritime operation unto itself during Operation Tomodachi. These two maritime forces maintain a great deal of interpersonal relationships with annual staff talks and bilateral exercises and the relief efforts of 2011 allowed these same relationships to foster an incredible amount of cooperation that I believe was to the detriment of joint bilateral planners within the Joint Requirements Review Board who was receiving requests directly from the Government of Japan. The fact that "USN-JMSDF integrated relief operations were moving so fast that the Japanese Self Defense Force, JTFC, and the CJTF To-Hoku called for an operational pause" should not be a desired action during a disaster relief operation.[116] Utilizing personal relationships and a history of interoperability should prove to benefit an operation such as a humanitarian relief yet it should never jeopardize or confuse the operational picture by exceeding the bounds of the military assistance mandates to render only complementary relief of the 'last resort'. I feel as though within Operation Tomodachi, U.S. maritime planners allowed these inter-service bonds to cloud to necessary inter-governmental connections between the U.S. relief community and the assets executing the relief missions.

---

[116] Cathal O'Connor, "Foreign Humanitarian Assistance," 159.

C.   U.S. SECURITY POLICY RECOMMENDATIONS

I believe that any potential policy recommendations should be geared toward addressing a perceived lack of awareness of mission as seen on occasion within humanitarian relief scenarios. Lacking direct guidance from the relief agencies determining actual need and assessing the likelihood of the U.S. military responding to such requests, military unit commanders with often times rise to the occasion and meet whichever need suits his or her needs best at that particular moment. In an attempt to increase this 'needs based relief' awareness I propose the following initiatives:

- Decentralized planning and operations cells within a disaster relief scenario

- The expansion of USAID OFDA Military Liaison Units to more locations and units

- A less rigid JRRB Process that attempts to account for the totality of humanitarian aid rendered instead of concentrating on individual MITAMs

- Require Military Unit Commanders to attend USAID OFDA's Joint Humanitarian Operations Course prior to assuming command

The steps would ideally lead toward increased awareness of the connection between assessing needs from a host nation prior to executing operations to render humanitarian assistance. I will now attempt to examine each of these recommendations individually as well as discuss possible movement toward implementation as well as the likelihood, in my eyes, of such movement.

First, I believe movement toward decentralized planning and operations cells within a disaster relief scenario would promote a greater sense of mission and an increased alignment of needs and capability within future disaster relief scenarios. Allowing each component or operational function of an operation to have visibility and input into the request for assistance process would facilitate increased understanding of the needs currently being met and the military operations currently underway to accomplish those tasks requested. Such a process within the land and maritime components within an operation may contribute to a more comprehensively accepted mission goal and accepted steps toward delivering the necessary and more importantly, the requested, disaster relief aid within such a scenario.

Second, the expansion of USAID OFDA Military Liaison Units to more units within a disaster scenario closely follows the first recommendation in that it attempts to include more commanders and units within the operational planning portion of the disaster relief scenario. Decentralizing the JRRB/MITAM process may provide more 'buy-in' from supporting units, as it would allow them to see much of the motivation for their deployment and operational tempo. I think the type of forward-deployed Military Liaison Units that were utilized in Indonesia in 2004 worked well for each uniquely different aspect of the humanitarian operation and allowed local commanders to source requests for assistance at a smaller, more immediate level that facilitated a more rapid response. Such a move would likely be supportable in future scenarios provided the commanders of smaller military units are well-versed and familiar with standing USAID-OFDA protocol and procedures. Increased education and awareness are addressed below.

Third, I recommend that OFDA planners examine their current JRRB / MITAM processes in order to find more comprehensive system that captures the totality of U.S. military assistance rendered within a disaster relief scenario. Understanding that a mere 48 MITAMs within a three week operation involving over 15,000 Sailors and Marines is hardly reconcilable, I would think that it the public perception of expending that degree of resources and man-hours should hardly be a positive optic when assessing the value of rendering assistance within a humanitarian relief operation. While the current process in largely motivated by determining eligibility for OHDACA funding, future JRRB processes can, I believe, receive larger input from supporting commands within a disaster relief effort that can document their man-hours, flight times, and relief supplies offered in order to form a more complete picture of the military's assistance.

Fourth and finally, I believe military unit commanders should be required to attend USAID OFDA's Joint Humanitarian Operations Course. Currently provided to military members on a purely voluntary basis, this week long course begins an inter-agency conversation on the roles and responsibilities of the military and USAID within a disaster relief role. Mandating such attendance within a training pipeline does not seem unreasonable and would surely benefit operational planners and commanders before they possibly encounter similar roles within the bounds of their operational tours.

D.   RESEARCH OVERVIEW

1.   Significance Revisited

This research remains important for a number of reasons. Regardless the outcome, the United States should maintain the ability to critically assess its operational history in order to maximize the efficacy of future efforts.

First, U.S. military planners should continue to operate within accepted international standards and norms regarding the use of military forces and assets in support of humanitarian response to natural disasters. Robust international guidelines exist for this reason and the United States should continue its leadership in the Pacific in accordance with internationally accepted standards of behavior.

Second, the acceptance of humanitarian aid is never guaranteed and its assurance rests largely on perception and strong assessments of need. Consistency of response remains the greatest asset the U.S. military can wield within the Pacific as it continues to shape its perception to regional allies in Asia.[117]

Third and finally, U.S. military planners are beginning to accept the budgetary realities that will define capacity and employment even as resources shift into the Pacific. Successive Quadrennial Defense Review processes will likely continue to emphasize the importance of expeditionary forces. Future renditions of disaster relief efforts within the Pacific theater will provide military maritime planners the chance to utilize inherent flexibility and mobility within the fiscal restrictions of a future force.

2.   Research Shortfalls

Within the process of this examination, I utilized two case studies that I felt best illustrated the deficiencies within Operation Tomodachi's maritime response. The efforts to provide relief in 2004 in Indonesia was by many accounts a resounding success and I completely support this assessment, as well as commend U.S. maritime planners for accurate assessing need and providing appropriate capability in accordance with stated U.S. guidance and international norms and standards. Within the examination of Japan's

---

[117] Steering Committee, "Position Paper on Humanitarian-Military Relations."

2011 disaster however, I made the conscious decision not to discuss any of the consequence management factors related to the disaster. The nuclear plant disaster within Operation Tomodachi did little to impact the level of responding U.S. maritime assets and if anything, further exacerbated the consequences of maintaining excess military capability within the areas impacted by either nuclear plumes or contamination.

Additionally, while the strictures of USAID OFDA's validation process are evident in its results, I feel as though there has to be a more effective method with which to encapsulate the totality of DoD assistance within a disaster relief scenario. USAID understandably wields the JRRB validation process as a method to justify the utilization of OHDACA monies yet I feel as though a larger, more encapsulating fiscal measurement is necessary within any critical glimpse at future operational assessments of disaster relief assistance.

3.   Areas for Future Study

I believe there are a number of fronts along which students would be able to explore in regards to disaster assistance within the Pacific Region. The likelihood for a multilateral humanitarian force that aligns with ASEAN directives remains a pertinent topic and one that will no doubt be discussed in the future as the United States continues its pivot to the region. Additionally, potential areas for cooperation exist within the South China Sea beneath the auspices of disaster relief and it could prove useful for some of the co-claimants of territorial areas within the region begin their cooperation along more benign lines such as disaster relief.

THIS PAGE INTENTIONALLY LEFT BLANK

LIST OF REFERENCES

Adinolfi, C., D.S. Bassiouni, H. F. Lauritzsen, and H.R. Williams. *Humanitarian Response Review: An Independent report commissioned by the United Nations Emergency Relief Coordinator & Under-Secretary-General for Humanitarian Affairs, Office for the Coordination of Humanitarian Affairs*: United Nations, (2005).

Anwar, D. F. "Indonesia: Domestic Priorities Define National Security." In *Asian Security Practice: Material and Ideational Influences,* edited by M. Alagappa, 477–512. California, Stanford University Press, 1998.

Banyu Perwita, and Anak Agung. "Indonesia's Defence White Paper 2003 and the Limited Capacity of Civilian in Security-Related Issues." *Lembaga Studl Pertahanan dan Studl Strategis Indonesia*, January 31, 2008. Accessed June 8, 2012. http://lesperssi.org/id/conference/workshop-mainmenu-6/6-civil-military-relation-13-october-2003/45-indonesias-defence-white-paper-2003-and-the-limited-capacity-of-civilian-in-security-related-issues

Biondolillo, S., and A. Widagdha. *A Public Health Assessment of Aceh Jaya*: Samaritans Purse International Relief, (2005).

Clinton, Hillary. "America's Pacific Century." Foreign Policy, November 2011.

Daniel, James Lt Col. "Operation Unified Assistance: Tsunami Transitions." *Military Review*, January-February 2006, 50–53.

Defending The Country Entering the 21ˢᵗ Century. Jakarta, Ministry of Defence White Paper, 2003. Accessed June 2, 2012. http://merln.ndu.edu/whitepapers/IndonesiaWhitePaper.pdf.

Defense of Japan 2011. Tokyo: Japan Ministry of Defense, 2011a.

"The Effectiveness of Foreign Military Assets in Natural Disaster Response." *Stockholm International Peace Research Institute*, supported by the United Nations Office for the Coordination of Humanitarian Affairs. Accessed June 2, 2012. http://ochanet.unocha.org/p/Documents/The%20Effectiveness%20of%20foreign %20Military%20Assets%20in%20Natural%20Disaster%20Response%20SIPRI.p df.

Elleman, Bruce A. "Waves of Hope – The U.S. Navy's Response to the Tsunami in Northern Indonesia." Naval War College, *Newport Papers* 28 (2007).

Feickert, Andrew and Emma Chanlett-Avery. *Japan 2011 Earthquake: U.S. Department of Defense (DoD) Response*. Washington, D.C.: Congressional Research Services, 2011.

Griffard, B.F., Kent Hughes Butts, and Col. Art Bradshaw. "Support to Civil Authority in Seismic Disasters: Regional Initiatives." *Issue Paper – Center for Strategic Leadership, U.S. Army War College* (February 2006, Volume 02–06).

Piombo, Jessica and Michael Malley. "Beyond protecting the land and the sea: the role of the U.S. Navy in reconstruction." In *Naval Peacekeeping and Humanitarian Operations*, edited by James J. Wirtz and Jeffrey A. Larsen, 61–80. New York, Rutledge, 2009.

Harkin, Clare. "The 2004 Tsunami: Civil Military Aspects of the International Response." *Tsunami Evaluation Coalition*, Coordination of International Humanitarian Assistance in Tsunami-Affected Countries.

Harvard Kennedy School Indonesia Program. "From Reformasi to Institutional Transformation: A Strategic Assessmet of Indonesia's Prospects for Growth, Equity and Democratic Governance." (2011).

Human Rights Watch. "Unkept Promise: Failure to End Military Business Activity in Indonesia." January 2010.

Human Rights Center, University of California Berkeley. *After The Tsunami – Human Rights of Vulnerable Populations*, October 2005.

Humanitarian Policy Group at the Overseas Development Institute, 2006. "Resetting the Rules of Engagement: Trends and Issues in Military-Humanitarian Relations." Accessed June 2, 2012. http://ochanet.unocha.org/p/Documents/Humanitarian%20Policy%20Group%20Report%20Civil-Military%20Coordination.pdf.

"Indonesia: The First Fifty Years." In *The Emergence of Modern Southeast Asia*, ed by Norman G. Owen, 431–447.Honolulu: University of Hawai'i Press, 2005.

International Federation of Red Cross and Red Crescent Societies, Opinion Piece. "Learning the Lessons from the Tsunami." Accessed June 1, 2012. http://www.ifrc.org/en/news-and-media/opinions-and-positions/opinion-pieces/2005/learning-the-lessons-from-the-tsunami/.

International Federation of Red Cross and Red Crescent Societies, Press Release published January 2, 2005. "Red Cross Red Crescent Relief Efforts Under Way in Devastated Aceh." Accessed June 2, 2012. http://www.ifrc.org/en/news-and-media/press-releases/asia-pacific/indonesia/red-cross-red-crescent-relief-efforts-under-way-in-devastated-aceh/.

International Medical Corps, *Japan: One Year Report*. Accessed June 2, 2012. http://reliefweb.int/sites/reliefweb.int/files/resources/PDF_203.pdf.

Jane's Defence Budgets. "Indonesia Defence Budget." Posted June 14, 2011. Accessed May 29, 2012. http://search.janes.com.

Japanese Red Cross Society. "Japan: Earthquake and Tsunami. Operations Update No. 1, April 13, 2011. Accessed May 3, 2012. http://www.jrc.or.jp/vcms_lf/JRCS_OperationsUpdate1.pdf.

———. "Japan: Earthquake and Tsunami. Operations Update No. 2, May 2, 2011. Accessed May 3, 2012. http://www.jrc.or.jp/vcms_lf/JRCS_OperationsUpdate2.pdf.

———. "Japan: Earthquake and Tsunami. Operations Update No. 3, May 20, 2011. Accessed May 3, 2012. http://www.jrc.or.jp/vcms_lf/kokusai_110523.pdf.

———. "Japan: Earthquake and Tsunami. Operations Update No. 4, June 29, 2011." Accessed May 3, 2012. http://www.jrc.or.jp/vcms_lf/kokusai_290611.pdf.

Johnson, Eric. "Operation Tomodachi a Huge Success, But was it One-Off?" *The Japan Times Online*, March 3 2012. Accessed March 9, 2012. http://www.japantimes.co.jp/text/nn20120303f1.html.

Kato, Kazuyo. *The Response to Japan's March 11 Disaster: When the Going Gets Tough...* Washington, D.C.: Center for Strategic and International Studies, 2011.

Kimura, Ehito. "Indonesia in 2010: A Leading Democracy Disappoints on Reform." *Asian Survey*, Vol. 51, No. 1 (2011): 186–95.

Kubota, Yoko. "Japan Red Cross Struggling to Hand Out Record Donations." *Reuters*, April 7 2011. Accessed June 2, 2012. http://www.reuters.com/article/2011/04/07/us-japan-aid-idUSTRE73638O20110407.

Martin, Alex. "Military Flexes Relief Might, Gains Newfound Esteem." *The Japan Times Online*, April 15 2011. Accessed March 9, 2012. http://www.japantimes.co.jp/text/nn20110415f1.html.

National Bureau of Asian Research. "Chronology of Operation Tomodachi. Amidst Trial, Ties that Bind: Enduring Strength of the U.S.-Japan Alliance." Accessed March 9, 2012. http://www.nbr.org/research/activity.aspx?id=121.

"National Coordination Agency for Disaster Management." President of Republic of Indonesia, Presidential Regulation Number 83 of 2005. Accessed June 2, 2012. http://www.gitews.org/tsunami-kit/en/E6/further_resources/national_level/peraturan_presiden/Perpres%2083–2005_Bakornas-English.pdf.

Schaar, Johan. International Federation of Red Cross or Red Crescent Societies. "Sustainable, Appropriate Reconstruction A Must for Tsunami-Affected Communities." Accessed June 2, 2012. http://www.ifrc.org/en/news-and-media/opinions-and-positions/opinion-pieces/2005/sustainable-appropriate-reconstruction-a-must-for-tsunami-affected-communities/.

Sebastian, Leonard C. and Iisgindarsah. "Assessing 12-year Military Reform in Indonesia: Major Strategic Gaps for the Next Stage of Reform." Paper presented at the S. Rajaratnam School of International Studies, Singapore, April 6, 2011.

Steering Committee for Humanitarian Response. "Position Paper on Humanitarian-Military Relations, January 2010." Accessed June 4, 2012. http://ochanet.unocha.org/p/Documents/Steering%20Committee%20for%20Humanitarian%20Response-%20SCHR%20position%20paper%20on%20humanitarian-military%20relations%20(2010).pdf.

Tanter, Richard. "Intelligence Agencies and Third World Militarization: A case Study of Indonesia, 1966–1989, with Special Reference to South Korea, 1961–1989." PhD diss., Monash University, 1991.

Telford, John and John Cosgrave. "Joint Evaluation of the International Response to the Indian Ocean Tsunami: Synthesis Report." *Tsunami Evaluation Coalition*, July 2006.

Tomsa, Dirk. "Indonesian Politics in 2010: The Perils of Stagnation." *Bulletin of Indonesian Economic Studies*, Vol. 46, No. 3 (2010): 309–28.

United Nations. "Regional Workshop on Lessons Learned and Best Practices in the Response to the Indian Ocean Tsunami: Report and Summary of Main Conclusions." Paper presented in Medan, Indonesia, June 13–14, 2005.

United Nations Office for the Coordination of Humanitarian Affairs. "Japan: Post-Earthquake Coordination Saves Lives. Accessed March 12, 2012. http://www.unocha.org/top-stories/all-stories/japan-post-earthquake-coordination-saves-lives.

———. "Guidelines on the Use of Military and Civil Defence Assets in Disaster Relief – 'Oslo Guidelines'." Revision 1, November 2006.

———."Asia-Pacific Regional Guidelines For The Use of Foreign Military Assets in Natural Disaster Response Operations." Draft Version 8.0, November 23 2010. Accessed June 1, 2012. http://ochanet.unocha.org/p/Documents/APC-MADRO%20Draft%20Guidelines%20V8.0%20(23%20November%202010).pdf

———. *Annual Report 2011*. Accessed June 2, 2012. http://reliefweb.int/sites/reliefweb.int/files/resources/2011%20OCHA%20Annual%20Report%20Final%20150dpi.pdf.

United States Forces Japan. "Subject – Establish A Joint Requirement Review Board (JRRB) for Operation Tomodachi." Date Time Group 192341Z MAR 11. Accessed March 9, 2012. www.pacom.mil/web/PACOM_resources/word/j46-Encl-(1)-ESTABLISH-JRRB.DOCX.

Weatherbee, Donald E. "Indonesian Foreign Policy: A Wounded Phoenix." *Southeast Asian Affairs*, Vol. 2005: 150–170.

Weidie, Scott A., CDR. "Multinational Crisis Response in the Asia-Pacific Region: The Multinational Augmentation Team Model." *The Liaison* – Center of Excellence Disaster Management & Humanitarian Assistance, Vol. 3 No. 3 (2004). Accessed May 18, 2012. http://coe-dmha.org/Publications/Liaison/Vol_3No_3/Dept16.htm.

White, Stacey. "Corporate Engagement in Natural Disaster Response: Piecing Together the Value Chain." *Center for Strategic & International Studies*, January 2012. Accessed June 2, 2012. http://reliefweb.int/sites/reliefweb.int/files/resources/120117_White_CorporateEngagement_Web.pdf.

Wilderspin, Ian. International Federation of Red Cross and Red Crescent Societies. "More Must Be Done to Save Lives in Disaster Zones." Accessed June 1, 2012. http://www.ifrc.org/en/news-and-media/opinions-and-positions/opinion-pieces/2005/more-must-be-done-to-save-lives-in-disaster-zones/.

Willitts-King, Barnaby. "The Role of the Affected State in Humanitarian Action: A Case Study on Indonesia." *Humanitarian Policy Group*, Overseas Development Group, February 2009. Accessed June 1, 2012. http://www.odi.org.uk/resources/docs/4006.pdf.